# Reading Biography

# Reading Biography

*Carl Rollyson*

iUniverse, Inc.
New York  Lincoln  Shanghai

# Reading Biography

All Rights Reserved © 2004 by Carl Rollyson

No part of this book may be reproduced or transmitted in any form or by any means, graphic, electronic, or mechanical, including photocopying, recording, taping, or by any information storage retrieval system, without the written permission of the publisher.

iUniverse, Inc.

For information address:
iUniverse, Inc.
2021 Pine Lake Road, Suite 100
Lincoln, NE 68512
www.iuniverse.com

ISBN: 0-595-33747-3

Printed in the United States of America

# Contents

Introduction .................................................................................vii

Chapter One: Authorized and Unauthorized Biography ...............1

Chapter Two: Boswell's Legacy .......................................................17

Chapter Three: Autobiography and Biography ............................24

Chapter Four: Fiction and Biography ...........................................31

Chapter Five: History and Biography ...........................................37

Chapter Six: Literary Biography ....................................................49

Chapter Seven: Brief Biographies ..................................................54

Chapter Eight: Innovative Biographies .........................................64

Chapter Nine: Comparing Biographers ........................................69

Name Index .....................................................................................99

Title Index .....................................................................................103

# *Introduction*

In the spring of 2003, I began to publish a weekly column, "On Biography," in *The New York Sun* at the behest Robert Messenger, the paper's Deputy Managing Editor, who was familiar with my work, and who believes that some of the finest contemporary writing is to be found in biographies. This is not a widespread view—that is, if one reads only the book reviews in newspapers, magazines, and journals. Novels, poetry, and drama generally receive more respect and more searching critical attention than biographies. That has been my perception as both a biographer and an avid reader of criticism published in Great Britain and the United States. So I have attempted to write a different kind of book review—one that did not merely discuss the subject of the biography or provide a sort of book report, with perhaps a sentence or two that praised or blamed the biographer.

Regardless of the publication, I have found that most book reviewers know very little about the history or the art of biography. Indeed, if there is any art in biography, it is the rare reviewer that acknowledges it or knows how to discuss it. Usually the reviewer regards biography as an occasion to wax eloquent about what he or she thinks of the subject. Little space, if any, is devoted to the biography's structure or style, to the biographer's peculiar problems, or to how the biography relates to others about the same subject.

I proposed, then, to write a column that reviewed a new biography each week while raising crucial issues about this literary form. I would draw on my experience as a biographer and a scholar of biography. I wanted to show, for example, the ramifications of authorized and unauthorized biographies, to investigate the relationship between biography and history, autobiography and biography, biography and fiction, as well as comment on certainly perennial biographical subjects such as Napoleon, or on subgenres such as children's biography.

In assembling this book, I have chosen those reviews that best seem to illuminate a vital aspect of biography. In this sense, the reviews transcend their occasion—that is, I am not just evaluating the biography at hand but reading it as a biographer and critic who is passionately devoted to a genre whose intricacies are rarely explored in the realm of book reviews and newspaper columns.

My aim is to reach not merely scholars but that vast general audience addicted to reading biography. I hope to enhance their pleasure by providing insight (or you might say, the inside word) on how biographies are put together. I am trying to combine my delight as both a creator and a consumer of biography.

As a classroom teacher, I want to use this book as a way to excite my students' interest in a genre that I regard as a unique form of knowledge—one that requires far more attention in the academy than it has been commonly accorded.

In closing, I would like to acknowledge *The New York Sun's* permission to reprint these reviews (all published in 2003-2004), which have benefited greatly from the editing of Robert Messenger and David Propson. Their continuing confidence in my work has been a wonderful source of inspiration—as has the editing of my wife, Dr. Lisa Paddock, my first reader and shrewdest critic.

# Chapter One

## *Authorized and Unauthorized Biography*

*Gellhorn: A Twentieth Century Life* by Caroline Moorehead

"The first major biography of Martha Gellhorn," Caroline Moorehead's publisher announces. So there is at least one minor biography? I hope readers will ask, for in fact there are two: "Nothing Ever Happens to the Brave" (1990) and "Beautiful Exile" (2001)—both authored by me, although I do not consider them minor. The first made Gellhorn furious; the second provoked a press campaign to discredit me, conducted on her behalf by friends in Britain. This sequence of events perhaps explains why neither is included in Ms. Moorehead's "sources and select bibliography." She has been authorized by the Gellhorn estate, and that means I have become the nonbiographer.

Martha Gellhorn is rightly described in the publisher's copy as having pursued a "heroic career as a reporter [which] brought her to the front lines of virtually every significant international conflict between the Spanish Civil War and the end of the Cold War." She was also Ernest Hemingway's third wife, the only one to walk out on him, and a fine writer of novellas, which Alfred A. Knopf published in a single fat volume a decade ago.

I learned a good deal about Gellhorn from reading Ms. Moorehead's book—chiefly how she viewed her own life—in letters that only her authorized biographer has been allowed to read. Gellhorn was more critical of herself than I had imagined, acknowledging that she put all her skill into reporting. She had a great eye and ear, but she had no gift for analysis. I knew that Gellhorn could only write about what she had seen and heard, and that she was no thinker, but I did not realize that she herself came to this same conclusion after fruitless efforts to complete books about the Spanish Civil War, Cuba, and Vietnam.

Readers of this column are already familiar with my method of inquiry: What is new in this biography? How does Ms. Moorehead handle her sources? How does her book accord with my understanding of biography as a genre?

First, Ms. Moorehead has had the unlimited access to the evidence and interviewees that every biographer seeks. I was delighted to see descriptions of Gellhorn's austere London flat, virtually a mirror of her astringent mind; to discover that she was very pleased with her long and narrow feet and had Ferragamo make shoes especially for her; that "new words made her laugh with sudden delight." From Plutarch to Boswell and beyond, good biographers have given us such details and anecdotes to make their subjects live again.

There is one source, however, that Ms. Moorehead studiously avoids. In her only reference to my biographies, she repeats Gellhorn's charge that my work is riddled with errors. Ms. Moorehead need not have trusted my books. By using almost any of the Internet search engines, she could have found my archive at the University of Tulsa, open to any researcher who wants to examine the notes, correspondence, and tape-recorded interviews I used in my two biographies of Martha Gellhorn. I eagerly read Ms. Moorehead to see what I got wrong, but her biography only confirms what I believed: that Gellhorn's charges had no merit. One of Gellhorn's closest friends, the biographer Victoria Glendinning, once told me that she doubted I had made errors and assured me that Gellhorn was just mad at me.

When she got mad, she lost all perspective. Gellhorn was mad at her own native land and lived most of her life away from it. She was mad at the Palestinians and would not brook a single word of criticism of Israelis. She loved the Spanish republic and never wrote one word about how the loyalists committed atrocities or how the Stalinists eliminated all elements of the left that did not hew to Moscow's line. She was a partisan in every sense of the word and was even proud of denouncing journalists who talked about that "objectivity shit." There was right and there was wrong and there was nothing in between.

Ms. Moorehead sees this side of her subject—but only selectively. Hers is one of the most anti-American books I have ever read. Ms. Moorehead repeats without comment every hysterical charge Gellhorn has made against the United States. The biographer is only dismayed when Gellhorn does not give equal consideration to the Palestinians or to the Germans, whom Gellhorn did not believe would ever create a democratic country.

As a biographer, I'm shocked at how little attention Ms. Moorehead devotes to Gellhorn's St. Louis background. True enough, the relationship between Gellhorn and her mother Edna is sensitively rehearsed, but Edna's work as a reformer in St. Louis and the manner in which that reforming spirit energized Gellhorn is not portrayed. Her grandmother, a provocative social reformer in St. Louis, is not even mentioned! Gellhorn conducted a life-long campaign to distance herself from St. Louis and hurt her mother terribly by giving no credit to the city's progressive ethos; Ms. Moorehead writes in the same vein—as if she were writing not a biography but completing Gellhorn's autobiography.

In general, this biography is out of tune with what made Gellhorn, for all her anti-Americanism, an American figure. It is out of sync with her effort not to sound American: I was astounded by Ms. Moorehead's reference to Gellhorn's "accent as unmistakably still of the American Midwest." No American friend of hers I interviewed heard any trace of St. Louis in her mature speech. On television she always sounded like a posh mid-Atlantic confection, combining British and aristocratic East Coast elocution. Perhaps she saved the Midwestern "drawl" to entertain her British friends.

Still, Ms. Moorehead does deliver the news—with much to say about Gellhorn's lovers, from Bertrand de Jouvenel to Ernest Hemingway to General James Gavin, and many more. Crossed off the list, however, is H.G. Wells—primarily because Gellhorn denied the affair and was "scrupulous," Ms. Moorehead asserts, about identifying her lovers. Maybe so, but H.G. said they did make love. Having done my own extensive research on this randy writer for a biography of Rebecca West, I see no reason to dispute his account.

Has Ms. Moorehead's work changed the basic shape and significance of Martha Gellhorn's life as I described it? I don't think so. And for that I'm grateful.

*Anthony Powell: A Life* by Michael Barber

"Inevitably regarded as the English Proust," wrote Norman Shrapnel in the Guardian, to describe Anthony Powell, author of the 12-volume "A Dance to the Music of Time." Put the emphasis on English, since Powell's individual works reflect an Anglo Saxon concern with eccentricity and social comedy—not with any profound probing of Bergsonian time.

Powell's work is pure joy to a biographer, since he revels in the genealogies of his characters and the intricate narratives of their lives. What his characters do in the aftermath of World War I, how they negotiate the rather flaccid period *entre-duex-guerres*, and how they behaved in World War II, is cause for endless speculation. In Powell, not all is revealed. His narrators, like biographers, are never omniscient.

It seems inevitable that Powell's one biography deals with John Aubrey, author of one of the first great English biographical works, "Brief Lives" (1667). Aubrey sought to be accurate and lively. His biographical sum-ups, read together, are not so different from Powell's social comedy. And Powell, a great Tory and ancestor worshipper, believed that in the end the interplay of personalities over time—not plot or an overarching theme—was paramount.

I salute Powell the biographer because he believed in primary research and often chided secondary-source biographers who did not do their homework. Novels were homework as well, since Powell saw fiction as imagination feeding on experience. Literary gamesmen and women could spend their lives, if they chose, hunting down the real-life sources of Powell's huge cast of characters. He wrote to friends and colleagues asking for help with his characters' social and professional backgrounds and worked diligently at getting his dialogue and settings just right.

Powell is less flashy than his contemporary Evelyn Waugh—and not as well known in this country—although the cumulative impact of Powell's work is more impressive, I would say, than Waugh's. Powell's relative obscurity (Michael Barber points out) is also due to his refusal to put himself forward. Unlike Waugh, in other words, he did not make a show of himself.

An example of Powell at his best is his novel, "What's Become of Waring?" set in the publishing world (Powell worked at Duckworth for nearly a decade). Waring, a travel writer, has gone missing, and his publisher's effort to enlist a biographer's help only makes matters worse.

Michael Barber, on the other hand, is no trouble. He is a delight to read—though he is perhaps best absorbed after dipping into Powell himself. Mr. Barber rarely offers plot summaries or even explanations of what happens in Powell's novels. But to read Mr. Barber is to be reminded of what fun Powell is.

And Mr. Barber is amusing in his own right: for example, addressing Powell's reticence and tendency to skip over matters that another autobiographer (Powell wrote four volumes of memoirs) would feel compelled to address. When Powell writes that he had a "lonely…but not unhappy childhood," the biographer comments: "It is natural to conclude that…he may have left something out."

Mr. Barber rightly sides against those who reject Powell because he chronicled the comings and goings of the upper classes. Of course Powell was a snob, although his biographer handles the subject and his critics quite sensitively. In my experience, everyone is a snob about something—whether it is bloodlines or the correct way to bake bread. The point is what Powell did with his snobbery, which was to expose the people he knew and imagined to hilarious scrutiny. After all, Henry James argued, one must allow the writer his donné. It is supererogatory to lament that Powell was not a paid-up member of the Labour Party.

Mr. Barber's command of his subject is remarkable, even though he is unauthorized and was denied access to Powell's papers, which await the ministrations of his official biographer. Reviewers make quite a to-do about this kind of issue, though in my view the question to ask is whether the biographer understands his subject and has access to enough material to write the kind of biography he proposes. Mr. Barber, who interviewed Powell for the *Paris Review*, has an impressive sense of what his subject wanted told and what he was determined to withhold. And it is often the case that the authorized biographer can provide more details but not necessarily more insight.

I like the feel of Mr. Barber's book, and the sense that he is aware of how to manage his own narrative. Thus he writes: "This is probably the place to summarise Powell's athletic record at Eton." Rarely does he succumb to that bane of biography, the "must have been" and the "reasonable to suppose," which are no more than oblique confessions of ignorance.

Sometimes the biographer makes his point without any comment at all—as when he juxtaposes these two comments as epigraphs to Chapter 6, "The Coming Struggle for Power":

> "The voice of the Tempter: 'Unless you take part in the class struggle you cannot become a major writer.'"
>
> —W. H. Auden

> "The real test of a man is the sort of woman he wants to marry."
>
> —Anthony Powell

To the politically engaged writers of the 1930s, Powell was an irrelevance, if not a reactionary.

Mr. Barber presents fascinating scenes involving George Orwell and Powell, who believed that the former, when they first met, would indeed reject him as a reactionary. Powell was an avid reader of Orwell's novels and also admired "Homage to Catalonia," in which Orwell exposed the Stalinists. Perhaps this partly explains why Orwell wrote, "Tony is the only Tory I have ever liked." Malcolm Muggeridge, a great friend of Powell's, thought that Orwell's politics were confused, and that he had more in common with Powell than he realized. Certainly Orwell would not be the first socialist to find in conservatism a crucial truth he could not quite bring to consciousness.

Mr. Barber has the same eye for detail as his subject. He knows that Orwell's wartime reaction to Powell in his father's full-dress uniform is telling: "Do your trousers strap under the boot?" Orwell, formerly a policeman in Burma, asked Powell. To Orwell's satisfaction he learned they did, and he remarked: "Those straps under the feet give you a feeling like nothing else in life."

As Mr. Barber reports, Powell thought Orwell wore "his shabby clothes with style, hinting at the latent dandyism revealed by his comment about the boot straps." Mr. Barber goes on to make an observation about a photograph of Orwell at Eton after a swim in the Thames that demonstrates how biography, too, can be a dance to the music of time:

> He stands nonchalantly on the bank with his hands in his pockets, a rolled towel under one arm, wearing a floppy sun hat and with an illicit cigarette stuck between his lips. Here, one feels, is another example of the debonair insouciance that made such an impression on Powell.

*John Fowles: A Life* by Eileen Warburton

Biographers kill (only in fiction so far as I know) for the kind of access Eileen Warburton has had to John Fowles, still best known for "The French Lieutenant's Woman" (1969), made into a splendid film starring Meryl Streep and Jeremy Irons. Ms. Warburton, a student of the novelist's work since the 1970s, freely draws on 50 years of Mr. Fowles's diaries and on several interviews with him and his friends.

Even more startling is the complete control the biographer had over her book's narrative. My eyebrows ascended when I read in her introduction that not only did Ms. Warburton's subject not interfere with her work, he did not even read her manuscript prior to publication! Other authorized biographers sometimes make a similar claim to independence, but they are either self-deluded or less than forthcoming about the subtle way their subjects influence interpretation and control access to key sources.

Mr. Fowles's behavior is so extraordinary that it is difficult not to believe that it goes to the heart of the man and writer he has become. Indeed, from Ms. Warburton's revealing narrative, we learn that his fiction has been a long struggle to understand himself and his own motives for writing fiction. If it has taken him a lifetime to understand himself, and if (as his diaries demonstrate) he has often made mistakes in judgment, if he often relied on his wife to tell him the truth about his writing, how could he deny the possibility that a biographer, immersed in his oeuvre, might disclose even more about the nature of his life and work?

Mr. Fowles himself implies as much in a letter, which Ms. Warburton uses as an epigraph to her introduction: "The truth about any artist, however terrible, is better than the silence....I know many writers fight fanatically to keep their published self separate from their private reality....But I've always thought of that as something out of our social, time-serving side; not our true artistic one." To which this biographer can only respond, "Bravo!"

But the skeptic continues to ask: Can a biographer get any closer to the truth than the subject himself? Take this sentence early on in Ms. Warburton's narrative: "A sensitive only child, the boy must have been aware that he was the object of very high expectations." The critic pounces: "Ah, the tell-tale 'must have been.' In other words, Ms. Warburton does not know." True enough, but who does? She could ask John Fowles, but is he to be trusted? He would only be remembering the long ago, and the biographer shows that, like many writers, Mr. Fowles embroiders and fictionalizes his past—sometimes without realizing that he does so.

In principle, though, Mr. Fowles does recognize his fabulations: "I don't see how the 'lies' we write and the 'lies' we live can or should be divided. They are seamless, one canvas, for me," he wrote in a letter. It is the biographer's job, then, to show how the canvas got made: Instead of characterizing biography as a poor approximation of truth, critics ought to lay off and realize there is no gold standard of truth that can be used to judge biography as a counterfeit.

I cannot remember ever reading a biography that so immersed me in the daily anguish of the aspiring writer. Halfway through this biography, John Fowles is hardly more than 30. He has published nothing and suffered rejections from several publishers. He has been tormented by a love affair with Elizabeth Christy, the wife of his teaching colleague, John Christy. He eventually marries her but insists that she give up her only child, Anna. Then he relents and attempts to conceive a child with Elizabeth, only to be devastated by the discovery that her fallopian tubes are blocked. Later, surgery proves useless, and Mr. Fowles is bereft.

Yet out of this horrendous record of failure and futility came his first and one of his finest fictions, "The Collector" (1963). This story of a demented young man who kidnaps a young woman so that he can have her completely to himself is clearly an extension of Mr. Fowles's own fantasies and his obsession with Elizabeth Christy. The novel's reception was a working out of another Fowles fantasy as well. He had always imagined that somehow he would escape his literary apprenticeship by bursting into print not just with a promising first novel, but with a masterpiece—or, as Ms. Warburton's chapter title puts it, that he would ascend "straight to the top of Parnassus."

In effect, this is what Mr. Fowles accomplished when he attracted the distinguished publishing house, Jonathan Cape. As Mr. Fowles explained to literary editor Tom Maschler, "The Collector" had emerged only after 15 years of dreaming about literary fame, while he wrote and shelved nine or 10 other novels. An international bestseller and critical success, "The Collector" was turned into a film notable for a stunning performance by Terence Stamp.

I have to confess that, for me, the second half of Ms. Warburton's biography is not as absorbing as her bildungsroman beginning. John Fowles successful is just not as dramatic as John Fowles struggling. His passion for Elizabeth dissipated, and his work became uneven. Critics are uncertain about big novels like "The Magus" (1965, revised 1977) and "Daniel Martin" (1977).

But Ms. Warburton shows that her subject has not forsaken his self-critical diaries or his view of fiction as a way of exploring his strengths and weaknesses. It is to John Fowles's credit that he has divulged so much of himself and cooperated with a biographer who is clearly his match.

### *Mythic Giacometti* by James Lord

Why is it that certain biographers feel that they own their subjects? Some years ago, John Richardson gave Norman Mailer a very hard time about permission to quote extracts from his superb Picasso biography. Mr. Richardson did not believe that Mr. Mailer did justice to his subject. The pronoun in the previous sentence is purposely vague. Is Picasso Mr. Richardson's subject to be protected against the wayward Mr. Mailer? Why should Mr. Mailer not have his say?

As a biographer myself, I find the Richardsonian use of copyright to censor Mr. Mailer reprehensible, although it is done all the time—it was done to me, as a matter of fact, when Mr. Mailer's agency requested a look at my biography of him before granting permission to quote from his work. I suspected censorship. No, I was told, but blind permission to quote from Mr. Mailer's work might be taken as an endorsement of my biography. What nonsense! To Mailer's credit, he put a stop to this sort of intimidation and said flat out that he had never refused anyone permission to quote from his work.

These memories are called to mind with the appearance of "Mythic Giacometti," yet another James Lord effort to corner the market on the remarkable artist. If you have read Mr. Lord's classic, "A Giacometti Portrait" (1965, revised 1980), or his elegant and comprehensive "Giacometti: A Biography" (1985)—not to mention Mr. Lord's many other essays and books on the master—I'm not sure this latest effort will impress. A good deal of the book echoes—indeed, sometimes it copies—passages from earlier work. Mr. Lord's thesis is tantalizing—that the artist is a modern Oedipus—but also rather portentous and pretentious.

Here is a sample sentence: "Destiny proceeds at its own pace, step after fateful step toward the finality from which it is born." Oh, really? Who has Mr. Lord been reading? The Greeks? I'm not sure. Either he is too deep for me, or he is beginning to write sentences full of gas. Nothing like this kind of sentence appears in "A Giacometti Portrait," which is a modest yet insightful picture of the artist at work on a portrait of James Lord.

So why did Mr. Lord feel called on to produce what is, at best, merely a précis or skeleton of his much better and longer biography? I suspect "Mythic

Giacometti" is a response to the competition, i.e., Laurie Wilson's "Alberto Giacometti: Myth, Magic, and the Man" (Yale, 2003). "Myth? I'll give you myth!" I can hear Mr. Lord exclaiming.

Read the second sentence of Ms. Wilson's book, and you will see it strikes at the heart of Mr. Lord's biography: "All his life he [Giacometti] was wrapped firmly in the folds of a glowing family myth—that his had been the best of all possible childhoods." You don't even need to finish the sentence to see that James Lord is in for trouble.

The closest Mr. Lord comes in his biography to Ms. Wilson's skepticism is this sentence toward the end of chapter two: "Perhaps his childhood had, in fact, been as happy as he always said." But the perhaps goes nowhere in the narrative, and thus one is not surprised to find in the latest paperback edition of "Giacometti: A Biography" this ringing endorsement from Alberto's youngest brother Bruno: "I am convinced that if Alberto had been able to read this biography, recalling to him in detail the course of his life, he too would have felt pleased. This book, born of a great comprehension of the artist by the author, is nearly an autobiography."

It is presumptuous—even of a brother—to make such a statement. There was a time when James Lord believed in biography as something other than autobiography. "But what you may think of your work," he tells Giacometti in "A Giacometti Portrait," "while it's important to you, is not necessarily important to other people, or even necessarily the truth." Giacometti's response is to shrug and to continue painting Mr. Lord's portrait. In its understated fashion, Mr. Lord's earlier book exquisitely delineates the divide between the artist and his interpreters.

Ms. Wilson has not written a better biography than Mr. Lord's; indeed, in some ways it is not as fine. But she has identified a singular weakness in Mr. Lord's approach, which is to replicate what Ms. Wilson calls the "family myth": "Discord seems never to have entered the Giacometti family," writes Mr. Lord in chapter three.

Ms. Wilson, a psychoanalyst and art historian who began her career as a sculptor, does not dispute the facts Mr. Lord presents but rather the dynamics behind those facts. Has there ever been a family—even the happiest—that did not, in some sense, experience discord? Surely Ms. Wilson has a right to be skeptical—psychoanalyst or no.

The trouble is that Ms. Wilson—wanting to overturn Mr. Lord—too often goes beyond the documentary evidence, which he obligingly pointed out to her in the course of an acrimonious correspondence in the Times Literary Supplement (November 14 and December 12, 2003). She speculates that observing the birth of his sister traumatized Alberto, but there is no proof that he did—

only circumstances that Ms. Wilson finds suggestive. Yet, as Mr. Lord remarked in his TLS review of her book, "a reader might almost believe Wilson herself had witnessed this birth."

But then Mr. Lord goes too far, claiming that because Bruno denies his brother could have witnessed the birth, that settles the matter. He castigates Ms. Wilson for constantly using phrases such as "I suggest," "I suppose," "I think," and "I believe." But in "Giacometti: A Biography," Mr. Lord, discussing his subject's first sculpture, finished when Alberto Giacometti was only 12, comments: "The other members of the Giacometti family must have been astonished by this sudden, aggressive burst of precocity." Obviously, the biographer does not know: Were they astonished? Did they perceive the act as aggressive? I'm afraid the idea that Mr. Lord stands on a rock of fact and Ms. Wilson on the quicksands of wild speculation will not do.

One aspect of biographers that is rarely discussed is thuggery. Not to put to fine a point on the matter, biographers are brutes. (By the way, in "A Giacometti Portrait," Giacometti says Mr. Lord has the face of a thug and a brute. The artist may be joking; then again, maybe not). Biographers meddle with other people's lives. In "A Giacometti Portrait," Mr. Lord confesses that he did not level with the artist; that is, Giacometti did not know that Mr. Lord was taking notes and documenting the portrait-making process for a book. Mr. Lord defends himself by saying he did not want the artist to become self-conscious. To be sure. But like any biographer, Mr. Lord was nevertheless manipulating his subject. That he has also made friends with Bruno and the rest of the family is beside the point—or rather is very much to the point because by now Mr. Lord seems nearly clairvoyant on the subject of Giacometti.

That ownership of Giacometti is the real issue for Mr. Lord is shown when he accused Ms. Wilson of copyright infringement in his review of her book. She had applied for but had been denied permission to publish reproductions of Giacometti's art, and yet Giacometti's art had appeared in her biography. Having experienced more than once this effort to kill a biography by denying permission to quote or reproduce the subject's work, I understood Mr. Lord's game. He admitted in his review of Ms. Wilson's biography that he had advised Yale not to publish her book, and then he sought to block her by using the copyright act as a form of censorship.

But would Yale actually risk a copyright infringement suit? Of course not, I immediately thought. But to be sure, I called the press and learned that nothing ever came of Mr. Lord's charges. And as Ms. Wilson herself explained in the TLS (November 14, 2003), the works she ultimately chose for her book were in the public domain.

The attack on Ms. Wilson is the fate of the outsider biographer, a role she emphasized by condemning Mr. Lord's assumption of "privileged insider status as the only route to truth." But then she damaged her own case with statements such as "Lord's limited grasp of psychological functioning prevents him from understanding my ideas about the complexities in Giacometti's response to the Second World War and the evidence of the Holocaust." First, Mr. Lord shows in "Mythical Giacometti" that he can be as psychological as you please (What he has to say about the artist's foot fetish would do Ms. Wilson proud). Second, if Mr. Lord is so incapable of grasping Ms. Wilson's precious arguments, where does that leave the rest of us who are not psychoanalysts or art historians or Giacometti adepts? Who is Ms. Wilson's book for?

But of course Ms. Wilson has let her anger get the better of her argument—an anger that perhaps began (I first wrote "must have"!) when Mr. Lord—as she relates it—told her face-to-face that "no one should write another biography of Alberto Giacometti—his was the only one that counted."

Both biographers walked away wounded from their clash over the subject they do not want to share. It is natural to be possessive about one's subject. But the answer to one biography is always another…and another. Try as any biographer might, he cannot lord it over all the others—Boswell excepted.

## *The Life of Graham Greene, Volume 3: 1956-1991* by Norman Sherry

This is not going to be one of those reviews that decry doorstop biographies. I promise. But surely comment is called for when the third and final volume of Norman Sherry's opus equals in size Richard Ellmann's "James Joyce." Even if we grant Mr. Sherry his conceit that Graham Greene is a great novelist, should this biographer's work be longer than George Painter's "Proust" or equal in length to Leon Edel's five-volume "Henry James"? Is Mr. Sherry in the same league as these renowned biographers? Does his method justify so many pages?

Mr. Sherry provides at the beginning of this volume a rationale for his epic size narrative:

> It would have been easier to have had a specific point of view, to have looked at Greene through a template of excessive admiration or excessive hate (and indeed one memorialist has done the former, one biographer the latter). Such a method dramatically reduces the scope of research that is ultimately undertaken, since conclusions have already been reached before the research begins. If one is ready-armed to see only what one wishes to see, truth is never served. Using such a method, one is not looking for the complicated man standing there but

only for the partial evidence which will either glorify or beggar the writer's view of the nature of the subject.

In other words, to be open to the subject's experience—especially to that of a writer who surely logged more miles in more parts of the world than any of his contemporaries—requires biography on an extraordinary scale. Mr. Sherry has himself become a fabled figure because of his willingness to retrace Greene's voyages to the ends of the earth (as the biographer did in his two well-received books on Joseph Conrad's eastern and western worlds).

But to whom is Mr.Sherry comparing himself when he refers to the hagiographical memorialist and the hostile biographer? I presume he has in mind Ronald Matthews, whose sycophantic memoir first appeared in France. An embarrassed Greene made Matthews agree to forego publication in English. Michael Sheldon is the only other biographer to complete a full-scale life of Greene, and given Mr. Sherry's animadversions on excessive hate,I had to take a peek at the competition.

Before I did, though, I reflected that I could not recall a case in which a literary biographer began by loathing his subject. Quite the contrary, it is more likely that the biographer begins with excessive admiration and gradually becomes disenchanted—or at least chastened to discover that his subject is not a paragon. Lo and behold, this is what Michael Shelden reported in "Graham Greene: The Enemy Within":

> When I began work on this biography, I intended it to be a very favorable portrait of a novelist who deserved all the prizes the world could give him. I wanted to trace each step of his career with sympathy and point out his virtues as both a writer and a human being. But along the way, I kept uncovering unpleasant facts, and my understanding of Greene's life and art gradually changed. I found a haunted character with many startling secrets, and I began to see that his work used an elaborate code to address these secrets. As more and more pieces of the code were broken, I realized that Greene was not the man he pretended to be, and that his work, too, has a disturbing underside to it, a side that reflected his personality even as he deceived us about it.

As an account of the biographer's psychology, I find this passage exemplary. And I have read enough of Mr. Shelden to know that he is no hater; rather, he came by the same hard, unsparing view of Greene and of humanity that the novelist himself possessed.

Struggling within Mr. Sherry's bloated biography is Mr. Shelden's Greene, crying to get out. Both biographers present a man and a writer who was one of the century's great deceivers—in the same league as his spook friend Kim Philby. In the face of all evidence to the contrary, for example, Greene continued to laud the Soviet Union and flatter Fidel Castro. There is a startling scene in Mr. Sherry's book involving a Cuban official who tells Greene to his face that a part of his movie script set in Cuba has to be censored. While Mr. Sherry does not shrink from such damning scenes, he backs away from them by discussing Greene's belief in disloyalty and duplicity.

Mr. Sherry contends that the only way for Greene to be his own man was through an act of betrayal. Greene spied for the British government but relished publicly attacking its policies. He made love to a woman, then told her part of his heart belonged to another. He engaged in this sort of two-timing repeatedly, and Mr. Sherry does not mind rehearsing episodes of his subject's recurring equivocations even when he recognizes that the reader—like Greene's lovers—wearies of them.

A beautiful Swedish actress told Mr. Sherry that she loved Greene but she was "too young" and he was "too cynical." I daresay anyone having to grapple with Greene would feel too young or too innocent—and, in my case, too American, as well. Mr. Sherry assures us that Greene was not anti-American, but I must say that if Greene was ever pro-American, he did a wonderful job of hiding the evidence.

What makes a novel like "The Quiet American" (1955) so disturbing and memorable is that Americanness is equated with a human tendency to delude oneself, to believe in one's virtue even while committing unspeakable atrocities. I do not like Mr. Greene's version of the American psyche, but I nevertheless find his novel haunting and beautifully executed.

America, anyway, is not the Great Satan in Greene's life and work. He could hardly live with himself, let alone others. His constant travel to France, Russia, China, Tahiti, the United States, Sweden, Jamaica, Mexico, Cuba, Panama, and many other parts—all the while setting his work in many of the places he visited—was, Mr. Sherry believes, connected to Greene's efforts to suppress a suicidal nature. Greene, one of the world's famous Catholic converts, loved to confess—not to priests but to lovers—and then to sin again. Indeed, his novels show an understanding of the tortured conscience that made priests want to confess to him. Mr. Shelden presented this Graham Greene in a stark and persuasive 400-page narrative, which Greene spent years attempting to thwart.

In his "Author's Note: Graham Greene and Biography," Mr. Shelden showed how Greene and his estate staved off would-be biographers, settling finally in the mid-1970s on Mr. Sherry as the official biographer who would tie up important papers, have exclusive permission to quote from published and unpublished work, and have first crack at interviewing many people who would be dead by the time another biographer was on the case. "History would be recorded, but it would be one writer's version," wrote the undaunted Mr. Shelden, whom I greet as a fellow old hand in the business of surmounting the barriers subjects and their estates erect to thwart the unauthorized biographer.

Greene chose his man well. Although Mr. Sherry exposes some of Greene's "less pleasant qualities," as Mr. Shelden put it, the official biographer nevertheless encases the unpalatable in a good deal of obfuscation about his subject's multiple selves and in Mr. Sherry's indefatigable efforts to travel to "Greeneland," as he calls it, and to unearth the originals or models for Greene's characters.

Evidently Mr. Greene knew his anointed biographer would spend decades on his detective work. In fact, a good deal of Mr. Sherry's to-ing and fro-ing occurred while his subject was alive. In 1985, novelist David Lodge observed that Greene "seemed to derive a mischievous glee from the tribulations that poor Norman Sherry had suffered in trying to retrace Greene's every step."

Indeed, if there is something heroic about a biographer who spends 30 years doggedly pursuing his subject, there is also something rather silly and futile about such elaborate exactitude. As Mr. Sherry concedes, the Greeneian landscape had changed by the time he arrived; it was not the world that the novelist experienced, although Mr. Sherry is adept at locating vestiges of Greenery (Greenish puns seem irresistible to whoever writes about GG).

Mr. Sherry comes no closer to the inner man than did Mr. Shelden, especially since the former writes schoolboy prose and employs clichés: the "initial shot across the bow in the battle of censorship"; "entered the lists to do battle"; "twists helplessly in the breeze." And there are other basic book-management problems. For example, there is a chapter devoted to analyzing similarities between Greene and the actor Paul Scofield. I fail to see the similarities or to understand why the biographer addresses an entire chapter to them. Indeed, Mr. Sherry is always asking questions because he cannot figure his man out—and how delighted that would have made Graham Greene (who, in fact, lived to see publication of Mr. Sherry's first volume).

On the question of Graham Greene's career as a British spy, Mr. Sherry cannot say any more, really, than Mr. Shelden. Both biographers are stymied by their devious subject, and by a British government that is not about to come clean on Greene—even if that government could really know what this faithless man was up to.

I use the word faithless advisedly. It is one Greene often applied to himself. If ever there was a subject who thwarted the very idea of biography, Graham Greene is he.

*Beautiful Shadow: A Life of Patricia Highsmith* by Andrew Wilson

There is nothing quite so satisfying as a big fat biography that is well told. Andrew Wilson gives us a book bulging with history, cultural commentary, and extraordinary access to a writer's diaries and letters—not to mention the testimony of countless witnesses to Patricia Highsmith's life. In part, the credit goes to the biography's subject, since she preserved this record of her life in the hope that a writer like Mr. Wilson would know how to exploit it.

In his introduction, Mr. Wilson gloats about his good fortune, noting that Highsmith & Co. dissuaded several contending biographers (likened to swooping vultures) from feeding on her life while she was alive. Almost giddy over his prize, the biographer confesses he had a dream about his dead subject in which she appeared and gave him the nod. A similar scene occurs in Henry James's tale, "The Real Right Thing," where the biographer is dismayed to discover that he has mistaken the hovering presence of his recently departed subject for approval when in fact he is being admonished to abjure his projected biography. Mr. Wilson considers whether his dream is only a "wish fulfillment," and in Jamesian fashion is chilled when he opens one of Highsmith's diaries to read her poem:

> Look before and look behind,
> There's still time to change your mind;
> Perfidy no time assuages,
> Curst be he that moves these pages.

Certainly Highsmith understood that biography is a transgressive genre, but then her own stories are about our affinity with the criminal mind. We are "seduced," Mr. Wilson writes, into identifying with Highsmith's most famous character, Ripley (about whom she wrote five novels), "until by the end our moral responses have been so invaginated, we are actively on the side of the killer, hoping he will escape punishment, as indeed he does, with increasing bravura, in each book."

Mr. Wilson has done something similar for biography, making his a bravura performance that seduces us into relishing all the confidential and secretive aspects of Highsmith's life. The parallels between the biographer and his subject are revealed when—long after the fact—he discovers the identity of a woman Highsmith had stalked after making a sale to her while working in a department store. Just like his subject, the biographer is a tracker; indeed, he learns more about the woman than Highsmith ever did, incidentally emphasizing the difference between biography and fiction. Highsmith imagined in a novel what the object of her fascination was like; Mr. Wilson interviews the woman's daughter to find out what the source of Highsmith's inspiration was actually like.

Mr. Wilson triumphs not only as Highsmith's biographer but as The Biographer, showing us why we read biography: It is, in the right hands, a continuation not only of the writer's life but of her work. Through her biographer Highsmith continues to write herself into the imagination of her readers. So gloat away, Mr. Wilson, for the joy you take in appropriating Patricia Highsmith's life is akin to the criminal gaiety she so treasured in Ripley.

Not the least of the pleasures of Mr. Wilson's book is learning new words—or so it was for me, having had to look up "invaginated" (to insert or receive, as into a sheath). The suggestive humor behind such a word indicates that the biographer can be as sly as his subject was in linking sex and crime in her tales of human passion. And Mr. Wilson informs us that Highsmith had a "dysphoric" familial history. In other words, she had an anxiety-producing youth because her mother was so unsympathetic—asking her 14-year-old daughter, for example, if she was a "les" and then telling her to "straighten up and fly right." Highsmith's stepfather (her mother divorced her birth father before Patricia was a year old) never earned her affection—indeed, by the age of 9, the future crime writer was fantasizing about ways to murder him.

Highsmith, born in 1920, grew up in a time when lesbianism was not merely considered abnormal and disgusting, but could not even be talked about in public when it was at the heart of Lillian Hellman's play, "The Children's Hour" (1933). As a result, Highsmith lived a kind of secretive, criminal life that made her hate and distrust society and revel in fictional characters who subverted notions of what is normal. Society is stupid, she thought, for believing that everyone thought the same way—or ought to. A Highsmith novel, then, is a sort of re-education, exposing readers to criminals and other characters whose vitality stems from their unconventional and even "perverse" behavior. Small wonder that Edgar Allan Poe was one of her favorite writers.

In an epilogue, the biographer returns to his personal engagement with the life of his subject. At first, I cringed when I read his seemingly self-indulgent account of putting on "Pat's old dressing gown." But then I thought of Highsmith's supreme creation, Ripley, now considered one of the great characters in modern literature. I remembered how Mr. Wilson made a point of repeating that Highsmith often spoke of Ripley as though he were a real person, and then I realized that Ripley, that master of assuming other people's identities, had decided to write Highsmith's biography. Has anyone checked to see if Andrew Wilson really is who he says he is?

# Chapter Two

## Boswell's Legacy

*Anthony Burgess: A Biography* by Roger Lewis

When was the last time you read a biography that confesses and enacts a passion for its subject? Over the course of more than 20 years, Roger Lewis came to see his literary hero Anthony Burgess as a fraud—but a magnificent one, whose work is worth reading not as the oeuvre of a master but as the vulgar output of a versatile writer gamely taking on Napoleon, Joyce, and Shakespeare. Indeed, for Mr. Lewis, Burgess took on the whole of the English language and European history and brooded spectacularly about the future in "A Clockwork Orange," the novel that became the film that made him famous.

Reading Mr. Lewis is rather like reading James Boswell in reverse, so that the biographer becomes not ennobled but exacerbated by his subject. As soon as you realize that Mr. Lewis is not going to let up on Burgess, you can relax. Forget about the idea of objectivity, of the biography "fat and worthy-burgherish on the shelf, boastful and sedate" (a quotation from Julian Barnes's "Flaubert's Parrot," which Mr. Lewis employs as one of the epigraphs to his book).

Who says biography cannot go negative? Doing so seems fair enough as long as the biographer announces his intention, as Mr. Lewis does in his bracing prologue. Just about every British reviewer of the book has blasted Mr. Lewis; in Britain, it seems, biography is still for the burghers.

Although this biography goes ballistic, Burgess emerges as an outlandishly attractive figure. The biographer captures his subject's robust command of language, his encyclopedic mind, and his maniacal drive to dominate the literary discourse of his time with novels, film scripts, book reviews, television appearances, lecture tours, literary festivals, distinguished professorships, translations, and virtually everything else that can make an author visible to the world.

In the end, it does not matter how many faults Mr. Lewis catalogs. Despite Burgess's bogus erudition, his pretensions about his status as a composer, and his decathlon-like pursuit of literary greatness, he remains an appealing, audacious, Dickensian figure, forever decrying the literary establishment that ignores him even as he pockets huge fees for appearances and publications. Burgess provoked high expectations that could never be fulfilled, but he brought to contemporary literature a magnificent horizon.

The question biographers are often asked is one they do not usually answer in their books: Why did you write the biography? But Mr. Lewis has the question in mind when he quotes, in another epigraph, Orson Welles's comment to one of his biographers: "I think there's no biography so interesting as the one in which the biographer is present. I think it's a wonderful story, the whole thing: trying to get me." "Get" is the key word here, implying both an attempt to portray the biographical subject accurately and to snag the suspect, draw up the charge sheet, and determine the number of counts in the indictment.

Like Boswell, Mr. Lewis first met his literary lion in distinguished company. Mr. Lewis was Richard Ellmann's student at Oxford when Burgess alighted there in 1985. The illustrious Ellmann, biographer of James Joyce and Oscar Wilde, became for Mr. Lewis a wonderful foil to the flamboyant Burgess. Burghers will be outraged at Mr. Lewis's irreverent depiction of his Ph.D. supervisor. In a squalid house Ellmann the Eminent makes a "meal of fetching gin and tonics," accompanied by a "plastic tub of what might have been called guacamole." The softspoken and diplomatic scholar will not joust with his jocular guest: "Tell me, Dick, which white wine did Joyce drink?" Burgess asks. "People come to blows over that," replies the evasive Ellmann.

Mr. Lewis's point, I take it, is that he will enter the ring with Burgess. Seldom has a biographer revealed in a biography that the biographer and biographee engaged in a kind of duel. This aspect of biography as blood sport is usually dramatized in fiction, or in the biographer's essay in reminiscence (where a few scores are settled). Yet out of this conflict comes the story, as Citizen Welles understood so well.

Biographers love to speak of their empathy for their subjects, but friction is required to get the machinery of biographical narrative moving. Like so many good pieces of writing, Mr. Lewis's does not depend on his opinions. Reject them, and you still have the engines of his perceptions driving you on to marvel at Burgess's mania. "The whole of English Lit. at the moment is being written by Anthony Burgess," the poet Philip Larkin wrote to a friend in 1966. And so it would be until the dynamo ran down in 1993, succumbing to cancer.

The key charge against Anthony Burgess is that he lacked feeling, and so his characters do not live. He is all contrivance, a confection, a counterjumper whose real name was John Wilson, once upon a time a modest, well-behaved school teacher who decided to use literature and a literary life to escape the responsibilities of being a real person. Thus his fiction does not reveal the man; it escapes from him. But in doing so the literary output becomes, like Las Vegas, a "genuine fake."

It is a romantic idea that we should identify with the biographical subject, a romantic idea that the subject is plumbing his own experience. It is more likely, Mr. Lewis proposes, that the subject is consumed in his work and becomes the embodiment of literature—of the tradition he has absorbed. Mr. Lewis is a contender, in other words, for the T. S. Eliot Distinguished Professorship in anti-Romantic biography, since he has done nothing less than shatter the mold of the genre.

*Governor Reagan: His Rise to Power* by Lou Cannon

Some of the best biographies are also memoirs. It is a difficult feat—to see a subject whole while providing a personal perspective. It took Boswell more than seven years to master this hybrid genre, factoring in the Samuel Johnson he knew for 28 years as well as other primary sources and competing biographies. This kind of biographer, committing his perceptions to a long gestation, can make his own developing understanding of the subject a study in itself.

Lou Cannon has been working on his own hybrid biography of Ronald Reagan for more than 35 years, developing an authority that his subject's authorized biographer, Edmund Morris, could only dream of in the outrageously titled "Dutch: A Memoir of Ronald Reagan" (1999). Mr. Morris referred to Mr. Cannon as "Dutch's most dispassionate chronicler." The phrase may not be meant as a demotion (chroniclers are not in the same league with biographers and historians), for elsewhere Mr. Morris acknowledged Mr. Cannon as Mr. Reagan's "longtime observer and biographer," but "Dutch" seemed designed to supplant not merely Mr. Cannon but every other biographer before and after Mr. Morris. As historian Joseph Ellis recognized early on, Mr. Morris took Boswell as his model—or as Mr. Morris told his editor, Robert Loomis, "I want to make literature out of Ronald Reagan."

Until I read "Governor Reagan: His Rise to Power," Mr. Morris's strategy of inventing himself as a character in Mr. Reagan's biography—as in fact one of Mr. Reagan's contemporaries—remained a mystery to me. The mystery began in 1997 when I was invited by the English Speaking Union to join a panel discussion among biographers, starring Mr. Morris. But at the last minute he pulled out, pleading the pressure of his Reagan biography deadline, and so his wife, the lively Sylvia Jukes Morris, biographer of Clare Booth Luce, appeared in his stead. She said not a word when I provocatively chided biographers for being rather stodgy, not inventive enough in constructing their narratives.

I had no specific remedies in mind—certainly not anything like Mr. Morris's radical departure from biographical decorum—but biographers on all sides attacked me as a revolutionary. I took the stillness of Sylvia the Silent as an even sterner reproof. But I now imagine she was sitting there musing on her husband's doomed attempt to "make literature out of Ronald Reagan."

Mr. Morris evidently wanted to play Jack Burden to Mr. Reagan's Willie Stark. The trouble is that this idea of the biographer as the subject's shadow works reasonably well in novels—in Robert Penn Warren's "All the King's Men" as well as in "Primary Colors," Joe Klein's knockoff of Mr. Warren—but it cannot work for biography. Mr. Morris was simply not there at the critical moments in Mr. Reagan's life. I can imagine Lou Cannon saying, in a paraphrase of Senator Lloyd Bentson, "Sir, I knew Ronald Reagan...." Perhaps this is why Mr. Cannon does not even include "Dutch" in the bibliography of his new book.

Mr. Morris attempted to deflect attention from his flouting of biographical conventions by arguing that Ronald Reagan could not be known through the usual techniques available to the biographer: The remote Mr. Reagan had no intimate friends and did not open himself up even to his children or entirely to his wife Nancy. But Mr. Morris went further, positing Mr. Reagan as a hollow man. This is a standard theme in Reagan biography. In "President Reagan: The Role of a Lifetime" (1991), Mr. Cannon himself made much of Mr. Reagan's career as an actor, positing the well-worn idea that actors are empty vessels: Having no well-defined personality, they take refuge in scripts and in characters who endow them with traits that they temporarily adopt while looking for other roles to play, ones that will fill the emptiness that otherwise haunts them. Mr. Morris, frustrated that he could not engage Mr. Reagan even after gaining unprecedented access to the White House, never got beyond this view of Ronald Reagan as actor.

The greatness of "Governor Reagan," Lou Cannon's fifth book on Mr. Reagan, is that it does. To be sure, acting is still an important theme in Mr. Cannon's newest biography. He recounts his interview with an angry Mr. Reagan who complained to him about accounts referring to him a "B-picture actor." Mr. Reagan named all the great actors with whom he had appeared in films and then, Mr. Cannon writes: "He calmed down, paused, and—almost shyly—added, 'I'm proud of having been an actor.'" To me, at any rate, Mr. Cannon has captured the tone of an engaged human being who conveyed his heartfelt conviction.

Paradoxically, this moment in Mr. Cannon's biography shows why Ronald Reagan cannot be explained solely in terms of his acting career—at least Mr.

Cannon does not seem to think Mr. Reagan was acting when he told his biographer what acting meant to him. Calling him just a "B-picture actor" is a way of demeaning Mr. Reagan's integrity, and Mr. Cannon has come to understand that Mr. Reagan pursued his jobs as lifeguard, broadcaster, actor, union leader, and politician with extraordinary integrity. Indeed, Mr. Reagan's belief in integrity was so deep-seated, Mr. Cannon reports, that he regretted agreeing to do the only film role that cast him as a villain. If Mr. Reagan was "only an actor," why should he worry?

Mr. Cannon has latched onto the greatest theme a biographer can have: explaining why his subject has been so misunderstood. Of course Mr. Reagan was a performer; of course he told the same jokes and stories repeatedly. But the idea that there was no thinking man behind the performance will strike anyone reading Mr. Cannon's account of Mr. Reagan's rise to power as absurd.

Mr. Cannon's work is so good that even the footnotes make compelling reading:

"I was interviewing Reagan for Ronnie and Jesse, the first of my five books about him. He had repeated so many passages of his autobiography verbatim that I was becoming frustrated and told him so. Reagan cocked his head and said, 'You want something new?' I nodded. Thereafter, in every interview over the next thirty years, he always gave me 'something new,' often a tidbit but occasionally a revelation."

It has taken Lou Cannon more than 35 years to put the tidbits and revelations together, but in the process he has corrected some of his earlier misinterpretations and drawn on such valuable work as Anne Edwards's "Early Reagan" (1987)—a wonderful source on Mr. Reagan's childhood and acting career and much better than her recent book on the Reagan marriage—and Garry Wills's "Reagan's America: Innocents at Home" (1987). I do not know if Mr. Cannon had time before publication to consult Peter Schweizer's "Reagan's War: The Epic Story of His Forty-Year Struggle and Final Triumph Over Communism" (2002), although Mr. Cannon's portrayal of Mr. Reagan as a union leader—one who loathed not merely communism as a political philosophy, but communists who used violence and deceit to manipulate unions and liberal public opinion—coincides with Mr. Schweizer's new findings.

Mr. Cannon concludes that Mr. Reagan had a mixed record as governor. But the evidence of the detailed narrative seems to make a more positive case: On the environment, on education, on welfare, and in the prudent management of public money, Mr. Reagan proved, after a shaky start, to be an outstanding leader. Especially eye-opening is Mr. Cannon's demolition of Pat Brown's reputation. This liberal governor believed himself to be Mr. Reagan's superior in every way, but after reading Mr. Cannon I am hard put to think of a single accomplishment of Mr. Brown's that Mr. Reagan did not equal and in most cases surpass. My only disappointment with Mr. Cannon's account of Mr. Reagan's governorship is that, except for comparing Mr. Reagan with Mr. Brown, the biographer does not provide a historical perspective for Mr. Reagan's gubernatorial record. Where does he rank among California's governors? I would still like to know.

Although Mr. Cannon does include significant material from his earlier books on Mr. Reagan, this is by no means a rehash. Both the tone of the book and the variety of new information mark an advance in understanding Mr. Reagan. Mr. Cannon's access to the governor's cabinet-meeting minutes is used to reveal, in most instances, Mr. Reagan as a decisive leader. (Mr. Cannon does not neglect to point out, however, that Mr. Reagan's penchant for delegating enormous authority to subordinates got him into trouble several times, as did his off-the-cuff comment about cutting down the ancient redwoods, a moment where he did, indeed, sound moronic.)

Best of all, Mr. Cannon has obviously studied himself as a biographer and has thought over the scores of interviews he had with Mr. Reagan and those close to him. Note the differences in tone among these three passages:

On October 27, 1964, a washed-up fiftythree-year-old movie actor named Ronald Reagan made a speech on national television on behalf of a Republican presidential candidate that had no chance to be elected.—"Reagan" (1982)

> A former Democrat who had become a Republican, Reagan was then a supposedly washed-up actor.
>
> —"President Reagan: The Role of a Lifetime" (1991)

> When Reagan burst onto the national scene with his speech for Goldwater...he was a political unknown. Even conservatives who were dazzled by the speech did not recognize that Reagan had been formulating it for a decade, most of the time as a Democrat, and that the ideas presented were his own.
>
> —"Governor Reagan: His Rise to Power"

One of Mr. Cannon's great contributions to Reagan biography is to show that the change from Democrat to Republican was not quite as startling as Mr. Reagan himself sometimes made it out to be.

I would quibble with the idea that only conservatives were dazzled by Mr. Reagan's 1964 speech delivered on nationwide television. I remember as a 16-year-old high school student watching Mr. Reagan on a black-and-white television screen. He did not make me a Republican, but I recognized the same sense of greatness that had thrilled me when later that year, as an exercise for an English class, I memorized and marveled at a speech by Franklin Roosevelt—a man who always remained, for Ronald Reagan, a hero.

# Chapter Three

## Autobiography and Biography

*Intertwined Lives: Margaret Mead, Ruth Benedict, and Their Circle* by Lois Banner

Biography reveals what autobiography conceals. The autobiographer portrays what Henry James called "the figure in the carpet," the unifying theme of a story—in this case an individual's life. In order to hone that theme, the autobiographer leaves a good deal out; even crucial facts get buried because they do not fit the pattern of a self-written life. The biographer, on the other hand, seeks what Leon Edel called "the figure under the carpet," the strand that appears like a refrain in the subject's life but the subject dares not disclose. Although Edel's conceit sounds distinctly Freudian, one does not have to be of that school to contend that autobiography is an exercise in repression.

I was reminded of this divide between autobiography and biography when I read this intriguing passage in "Intertwined Lives":

> A public figure of note, Mead wanted to write a memoir that would last. She also wanted young people to read it, for in the 1970s, when she was writing "Blackberry Winter," she had positioned herself as an intermediary between the younger, rebellious generation and their more conservative elders, and she wanted both groups to know about her parents' progressive child-rearing techniques—how they had raised several generations ahead of her time. Yet in a draft introduction to the autobiography that was omitted from the final version, Mead suggested that organizing it in terms of her parents' child-rearing practices wasn't her original plan. Rather, she had initially intended to chart the development of her sexual identity and to end a "forty-year silence on the subject." Draft chapters on her childhood focus on her participa-

tion in the culture of romantic friendships between girls, although much of that material was eliminated from the published version.

As Jane Howard commented in "Margaret Mead: A Life" (1984), "Blackberry Winter" is an "evasive" book, which "asked nearly as many questions as it answered." What accounts for this autobiographical act of erasure, which the biographer detects as a gap in the story?

Ms. Banner tells us more than once: "From her early years on Margaret had a fear of being exposed, and by the late 1920s the possibility of exposure was real." Wanda Neff's novel about Mead and Ruth Benedict and their bisexual circle at Columbia University was published in 1928, and there were "rumors that Margaret was homosexual." Edward Sapir, an important anthropologist and one of Mead's disgruntled lovers, was mounting an attack on her work, but like other male anthropologists he was also spreading the word about her "free love" activities, which had flourished with Benedict.

Both Benedict and Mead were eager to get on in a male-dominated world. They were ambitious for themselves and for the new discipline of anthropology, which Franz Boas had established at Columbia. And they stood virtually alone as the two female stars who had crossed over from their own field and caught the public's imagination.

In "Coming of Age in Samoa: A Psychological Study of Primitive Youth for Western Civilization" (1928), Mead viewed the American adolescent through the prism of another culture, giving Americans perspective on their individual experience. She attempted to demonstrate that social environment shapes a society's ideas of what adolescence means. In other words, neither race nor human nature could explain the differences in society; rather, the concept of culture itself was the determining factor in an individual's life. As Benedict put in the preface to her equally famous and groundbreaking book, "Patterns of Culture" (1934): a people's culture is an integrated whole, a "personality writ large." Human beings are moulded by custom, not instinct, and society and the individual are not antagonistic but interdependent.

There is no gainsaying that Margaret Mead did much to make her own culture critically examine its assumptions not only about sex and adolescence, but about race and ethnicity. Yet, as her autobiography shows, she held back from publicly articulating the very idea around which her life had been organized, an idea that is implicit in her Samoa book: The practice of free sexuality facilitates the transition to adulthood and leads to contented marriages. Mead had three marriages and countless affairs, but they were not the painless experiences she breezes over in "Blackberry Winter."

Mead (1901–78) came of age in the free love 1920s. She absorbed and enacted notions of individual liberation borne by Benedict (1887–1948) a generation earlier. Benedict became Mead's mentor, companionate lover (to use a 1920s term), and loyal colleague, even as Mead pursued a professional and personal life that intertwined with other women and men. Benedict had carefully constructed a mask in order to make her way in a chauvinistic heterosexual world—a mask that Benedict's admirer, the psychologist Abraham Maslow, dubbed "the Benedictine enigma." In the early 1920s, Mead seemed destined to shuck off the mask.

But something happened at the end of the 1920s that scared both women and made them realize they would never be able to utter in public the very words, free love, that meant so much to them. They could see how the culture was turning against them when books like Floyd Dell's "Love in the Machine Age" (1930) began appearing. A former Greenwich Village radical turned conservative who attacked free love as "infantile," he received only the mildest rebuke in Mead's review in the New York Evening Post.

Mead's failure of nerve is understandable, and certainly Benedict counseled circumspection for women who wanted to succeed in academia or in the larger forum of public opinion. But in the 1970s, when it would have been possible for Mead to once again have a profound impact on her public, she glimpsed that possibility and withdrew like a Benedictine enigma.

This story is embedded in the heart of Lois Banner's dual biography, but there is too much detail here—as well as a defensive posture that sees the dilemma of intertwined lives almost exclusively through her subjects' eyes. One longs for a Jane Howard sentence that interweaves the claims of autobiography and biography: "She was loving, scolding, ebullient, irksome, heroic, and at times vindictive." A biography ought to have a few hard edges; Ms. Banner's seems all too yielding.

I wish the biographer had stuck closer to the story of why Mead ended up writing such a conventional autobiography, and how she concluded her life by taking refuge in the same reticence that Ruth Benedict regarded as essential to her survival. I wish Ms. Banner had done more intertwining instead of spending easily a hundred pages too many reprising the careers of these two women.

*Giving Up: The Last Days of Sylvia Plath* by Jillian Becker
*Her Husband: Hughes and Plath—A Marriage* by Diane Middlebrook

There are writers who want to be known for themselves, and not just for their work. Sylvia Plath was one of them. In "The Bell Jar," in her journals, in her stories, and in much of her poetry, her art and her life suffuse each other.

From memoirs like Jillian Becker's recent "Giving Up: The Last Days of Sylvia Plath," we learn how many of her intimate traumas she shared with her friends. This was an aspect of Plath that her husband Ted Hughes never understood. It would continue to perplex him when the biographers came calling. In the recently published "Her Husband: Hughes and Plath—A Marriage," Diane Middlebrook reports that Plath sent Hughes's love letters to her mother, who served as a kind of archive for all kinds of papers her daughter entrusted to her. After Plath died, her shocked husband protested his mother-in-law's plan to edit and publish those letters, which he deemed very private and "somewhat sacred." Indeed, he could never reconcile himself to the invasion of privacy that his wife courted, though at the hour of death he sanctioned publication of his counter-Plath poems, the "Birthday Letters" (1998).

In "The Silent Woman" (1993), Janet Malcolm's love letter to Hughes, she attempted to make the Plath biographies an appalling assault on a woman who could not speak for herself, with Hughes cast as his late wife's tormented guardian. But Ms. Malcolm's book—for all its brilliance, for all its perceptive probing of biography's failings—misfires precisely because Plath did not believe she could ever be silenced.

Instead, Hughes was forever trying to edit Plath or reinterpret her. Shortly after her death, he called up Ms. Becker, who had seen her the day before she died; he wanted to know what his wife had said. And Hughes kept calling, but each time failed to listen to Ms. Becker's words, instead trying to fit them into his own Plath myth. He kept repeating, without explanation, "It was her or me." His attempt to recast his wife was understandable as an act of self-preservation, of course, but it also reveals why his and Ms. Malcolm's barrages against biographers are so misguided. Hughes's behavior calls to mind Arthur Miller's efforts to refashion Marilyn Monroe in his play "After the Fall" and in his autobiography, "Timebends."

And now we have a film, "Sylvia," just out on DVD. It is a sorry thing. Poor Sylvia, she could not write as fluently as her Teddy boy. She baked cakes when she should have been penning poems. She gassed herself because she could not have him to herself. Poor Sylvia. The film is such a farrago of half-fact and simplistic psychologizing—not to mention that gratuitous nude scene with Gwyneth Paltrow perched on a sofa, bereft because Ted has abandoned her for the pregnant Assia.

A fully satisfying biography of Plath has yet to be published. This truth is less an indictment of her many biographers than an acknowledgment of how difficult it is to portray a life as protean as Plath's. Diane Middlebrook has made a good start on expanding our comprehension of Plath's pervasiveness. What is astounding about Plath is her relish of multiple roles. But the biographies present her as a mass of contradictions—feminist and subservient wife, high-art poetess and hack writer, the Mademoiselle who wrote potboilers (a term the Plath character uses for "The Bell Jar" in "Sylvia").

The filmmakers, like her biographers, are simply parroting what her contemporaries said about her. Susan Sontag, a member of the same generation, lamented in an interview that Plath felt obliged to seek popular attention so cravenly. Plath, however, viewed literature as a campaign to be fought on all fronts. The extraordinary point about her is that she was open to all forms and levels of literature. She regarded all writing as human expressiveness; she embraced it with Whitmanesque fervor.

I happen to have written a biography of Marilyn Monroe, and I was particularly struck by a Plath journal entry that seems show a rare insight into Monroe and into the role of a certain kind of literary figure in our culture, but also to reveal Plath's own unique stature, that which has made her a cynosure for a holistic sensibility no other writer has been able to bring off as completely. In mid-September 1959, Plath mentions reading Arthur Miller, and about two weeks later she records:

> Marilyn Monroe appeared to me last night as a kind of fairy godmother. An occasion of "chatting" with audience much as the occasion with Eliot will turn out, I suppose. I spoke, almost in tears, of how much she and Arthur Miller meant to us, although they could, of course, not know us at all. She gave me an expert manicure. I had not washed my hair, and asked her about hairdressers, saying no matter where I went, they always imposed a horrid cut on me. She invited me to visit her during the Christmas holidays, promising a new, flowering life.

Only Sylvia Plath dreams of audiences with Marilyn Monroe and T.S. Eliot, divining in her dreams that both are necessary. Like Monroe, Plath sought to fashion a persona that put her on a level with everyone—with readers of popular magazines and of literary journals.

Remember the scene in "The Seven Year Itch" where, as Marilyn and Tom Ewell leave a movie theater, she expresses her compassion for the creature from the black lagoon? If only he had had a little love. Plath, among other things, saw the domestic side of this icon, who wanted to do for her man, her Arthur Miller, while exuding both a motherly and sexy aura (see, for example, "River of No Return," or that scene in "The Misfits" when Montgomery Clift rests his head on Marilyn's lap).

Ted Hughes plays the Miller role in Plath's myth of her own life. Like Miller with Monroe, Hughes at the outset of his marriage to Plath was a pillar of strength, a serious artist whose attention to his wife increased her significance. Like Miller, Hughes shared his wife's dreams of fame and fortune. After Plath died, Hughes tended to deny this side of himself, and his British friends abetted his apostasy. Hughes told Jillian Becker that everyone hated Plath. He had in mind his circle of friends who found her vulgar—or as the bitter Hughes put it more obliquely to Ms. Becker in the days after Plath's death, his wife made him into a "professional," by which he seems to have meant she made him calculating and made him think about his "career," rather than allowing him to keep his amateur status as a chap who just wrote poems.

The flaw here, however, is that both before and after meeting Plath, Hughes was forever dreaming up get-rich-quick schemes. Until he was 12, he mostly read comic books, and as a well-established poet he still hoped to sell his children's stories and beast fables to Walt Disney. In "Birthday Letters," Hughes fleetingly acknowledges the kind of mythic pan-democratic union he had been forging with Plath:

> You were a new world. My new world.
> So this is America, I marveled.
> Beautiful, beautiful America!

Given the opportunity, I would write a biography of Plath that demonstrates that Hughes left her because he was incapable of matching the full kind of life she imagined for herself as mother, lover, wife, novelist, poet, and cultural symbol. Like Marilyn Monroe, Sylvia Plath wanted it all. Jillian Becker expresses great anger at Plath because she did not think more of her children, preferring instead a suicide designed to appeal to posterity. It was that Plath that the "very private" Hughes could not love or control, any more than Arthur Miller could control Marilyn Monroe, whose ambition Norman Mailer rightly deemed Napoleonic.

Like Marilyn Monroe, Sylvia Plath went to her death in a strange state of elation and despair that most human beings cannot begin to fathom. I remember listening to several hours of an interview with Monroe recorded just weeks before her death. I have never heard a more robust or vibrant voice, or a heartier laugh—it contained nothing like the screen breathiness that Jacqueline Kennedy Onassis imitated. Yet I know that sometimes on those same days Monroe would also plunge into deep despair. These lows and highs had to do with a sensibility that had been stripped bare of its illusions. Neither Arthur Miller nor any other man could rescue her—and yet she continued to dream of a "new, flowering life."

On the last day of her life, Sylvia Plath left Jillian Becker's house "invigorated, mildly elated, as I'd seldom if ever seen her before." As Ms. Becker's husband drove Plath and her children home to her cold London flat, she began to weep—as did her children—and he urged her to return with him. But Plath recovered herself and insisted she wanted to go home. The last person to see her was the tenant in the flat below her. She asked him for stamps and then stood in the hallway. Her disconcerted neighbor asked if he could do anything else for her.

(Gwyneth Paltrow captures the look of ecstasy on Plath's face as she tells him that she has just had the most beautiful dream.) And then Plath went upstairs and made preparations for death—putting her head all the way into the oven to make sure she could not be revived.

It may seem perverse—and at the very least paradoxical—to say that by her suicide Plath found the final way to recover herself. By all accounts, including her own, she had been writing great poetry, the poetry that would make her reputation, but she knew that no human being could sustain such a peak of perfection and perform all the normal functions of existence in the "kitchen of life," as Martha Gellhorn used to call it. When Sylvia Plath put an end to herself, she was at one of those crisis points when she was both exhilarated and exhausted by all she had accomplished. This is the state of beatitude, Shakespearean in its sublimity, which recalls what Menenius said of Coriolanus: that he had a nature "too noble for this world."

# Chapter Four

## *Fiction and Biography*

Why read fictionalized biographies—or watch docudramas, for that matter? Readers and viewers are disturbed when fiction melds with fact. What to trust? I asked this question myself when I read Jerry Stahl's "I, Fatty," an engaging effort to recreate the rise and fall of Roscoe Arbuckle, one of Hollywood's greatest filmmakers—a term I choose deliberately, because Arbuckle did much more than play the funny fat guy; he wrote and directed as well.

In the novel, Arbuckle takes credit for introducing Buster Keaton to the cinematic art. Is this Fatty, the unreliable narrator, making more of his influence than the facts warrant? Is this Mr. Stahl aggrandizing his character? To satisfy my curiosity I turned to Marion Meade's superb "Buster Keaton: Cut to the Chase: A Biography" (1995): "In Keaton's career, there would be only one artistic influence—not Griffith, not Sennett, not Chaplin, but Arbuckle." Reading Ms. Meade, I saw that Mr. Stahl actually underplays Arbuckle's violent temper—or is it the character, who like every autobiographer cannot see how his story conceals as much as it reveals?

Similarly, is it the bulky Arbuckle (he weighed close to 300 pounds) or Mr. Stahl who does not see that the Arbuckle scandal (he was tried three times—unjustly—for allegedly raping and crushing to death actress Virginia Rappe) was linked in the public mind with what Ms. Meade calls "an undercurrent of kinkiness" in his films?

Mr. Stahl does not include Ms. Meade's work in his bibliography, so I do not know if he consulted it. It might have done him good to read sentences such as: "A revolution in manners and morals was creating a younger generation whose behavior seemed, to their parents, absolutely depraved." "I, Fatty" sometimes lacks social/historical context, but then that is one liability of using a first-person, self-exculpating narrator. "What was said to have happened to Rappe was every mother's nightmare," writes Ms. Meade, who then quotes silent screen actress Lina Basquette, only 15 when the trials commenced: "My mother snatched the newspapers away from me. Those stories were not proper for me to read."

Like all good fictionalized biographies, Mr. Stahl's makes the reader reconsider the facts and speculate about what is missing from the record. How could Arbuckle have allowed himself to become mired in such compromising circumstances? Without placing undue blame on others, the Fatty of this novel shows how: He began life,in his father's eyes, as a criminal, one whose very birth ruined his mother's health.

Novels and films often focus on a single traumatic event—let's call this the Rosebud phenomenon, in honor of "Citizen Kane," one of the greatest fictionalized biographies. The conceit of Peter Stephan Jungk's novel, "The Perfect American," a fictionalized biography of Walt Disney, is that the town of Marceline, Mo., is Walt's Rosebud, the place he would re-imagine in his vision of a wholesome America and re-create in nostalgic theme parks like Disneyland. There is a stunning scene in this novel, in which Walt has to repair the Abraham Lincoln doll: an "electric scarecrow...much more lifelike than, say, the wax dolls at Madame Tussaud's. The surface of its rubber cheeks began to sweat and glisten under the heat of the spotlights. All its limbs were movable, the head alone was able to perform eighteen separate movements, the body forty-nine [probably more than our stiffer presidents could manage]."This doll can shift its weight and coordinate gestures in sync with some of Lincoln's memorable words.

I saw this automaton in action 35 years ago on a trip to Disneyland, and I did find it a marvel—much more appealing than seeing an actor play the president. Disney believed that technology could bring us nearer to the past, to the world of Marceline, and to American values worth preserving. In the novel, he is the only one who can control the doll, which is still in development. But then it attacks Walt, and he barely escapes serious injury. Both the grandeur and the self-defeating aspects of Disneyism are on display.

Of course no such scene ever took place—or at least I presume not. In this case I did not bother to measure Mr. Jungk's fiction against the facts. The book is narrated by Wilhelm Dantine, a disgruntled ex-employee whose life is, he believes, ruined and repossessed by "Uncle Walt," who has, he says, taken credit for all the drawings and scripts and even ideas that animators like Dantine (Disney liked to call them imagineers) created. So again we have the problem of an unreliable narrator. But to me, this novel seems to be about the metaphorical nature of Disney, and not so much an effort to fill in gaps in the Disney biographies or to dramatize what is already known about Disney's life.

Several years ago I reviewed Mr. Jungk's innovative biography of Franz Werfel, the Austrian author of "The Song of Bernadette," who was also a Hollywood denizen. The book had an interesting method: At the end of each chapter italicized passages, written in the present tense, showed the biographer interacting with his interviewees, listening to their contradictory or incomplete stories, and marking the changes in time—comparing Prague and the Vienna of the 1990s with those of 40 years earlier. In such passages, the biographer dramatized biography as a work of history while at the same time identifying the gaps in his knowledge, the areas closed to his investigation, the moments when one interview faltered, the occasions when another interview elicited an energetic, almost hectic counterpoint to the calm, well-ordered narrative of the chapters themselves.

Wilhelm Dantine does much the same in this novel, except that unlike Mr. Jungk, the biographer, he is freer to reimagine scenes that others have told him about. In Dantine's hands, biography also becomes an act of revenge, demonstrating that animosity can yield truths just as important as those brought about by the biographer's empathy for his subject. Wilhelm Dantine (WD) becomes his subject's alter ego, the Hyde to Walt Disney's Jekyll.

Many readers remain skeptical of fictionalized biography. After Robert Penn Warren sent William Faulkner "All the King's Men" (based on Huey Long's life), the latter replied that Warren should have thrown it away, except for the novel-within-a novel, the haunting story of Cass Mastern, an entirely fictional creation who is the subject of narrator Jack Burden's doctoral thesis. Faulkner believed that including historical figures—or even characters drawn on such figures—debased fiction. After all, you can quarrel with Warren's interpretation of Huey Long, but no one other than Faulkner can be an authority on the Snopes family.

In "The Historical Novel," Georg Lukacs argued that Sir Walter Scott's novels solved the kind of problem Faulkner identified by making major historical figures minor characters while using minor or invented historical figures as major characters. Thus Scott could provide a narrative of the period, explaining the context in which its principal actors appeared without hazarding examination of, for example, James Stuart, pretender to the throne of England, who is given a minimal number of words to speak in a novel like "Redgauntlet" (1824).

Writers with less reverence for history, who see history itself as a kind of fiction, or who see fiction as the supreme creation capable of subsuming facts for a higher truth, might side with E. L. Doctorow, who when asked if Emma Goldman and Evelyn Nesbit ever met—as they do in "Ragtime"—replied, "they have now." A less playful writer than Mr. Doctorow might have handled the question differently: "Look it up."

Far more interesting to me is the interplay between biography and the novel. It is a two-way street, you know. When New Republic reviewer Lee Siegel observed that Joyce Carol Oates's "Blonde" was indebted to my biography of Marilyn Monroe, I turned to Ms. Oates's pages to see if she mentioned me.

Indeed, she did. Like Jerry Stahl, she appends a bibliography and a commentary on her novel. Her way of integrating Monroe's movies as events in her biography, and her dramatization of Monroe's acting not so much as an expression of her subject's personality but as an active shaper of it, agreed with my reading of Monroe's life.

I also saw that in at least one respect Ms. Oates had surpassed me. Her evocation of Monroe's childhood is haunting. The novelist creates scenes—more than could be done with fact alone—in which Monroe's harrowing encounters with her violently unstable mother create a disequilibrium. If I were to write my biography of Monroe again, I know that the level of my engagement with Monroe's childhood would be much greater because I have read Ms. Oates.

This is pertinent to the point Mr. Stahl makes about his character's childhood in "I, Fatty." It is not insignificant that the title of his novel evokes, "I, Claudius," one of the greatest of fictionalized biographies. Mr. Stahl, by having Arbuckle tell his own story, and Mr. Jungk, by injecting a new voice into the Disney saga, emphasize the truth of the truism that biography is never the whole story. But then neither is the novel. You need one to complement the other.

*The Blood Doctor* by Barbara Vine

Biographers seldom take their readers into their confidence, even though, as the biographer and historian Paul Murray Kendall once wrote, all biography is autobiography. We do not turn to biography to read about the biographer. And yet, who tells the story is of vital importance. Norman Mailer recognized this fact when interweaving a few of his own fantasies into his biography of Marilyn Monroe. While Mr. Mailer can be accused of self-indulgence, in fact he was declaring an interest. The drama of a biography, he realized, consists in the writer's interaction with his subject.

In order to understand the biographer, writers often resort to fiction—as Barbara Vine (Ruth Rendell) does brilliantly in her new novel "The Blood Doctor." The novel is, in effect, the autobiography of Martin Nauther, a professional biographer who is researching the life of his great-grandfather, Lord Henry Nauther, one of Queen Victoria's physicians (she made him a peer) and an eminent authority on hemophilia. Martin has inherited Henry's seat in the House of Lords, and Martin's life, like his greatgrandfather's, becomes suffused with a consciousness of blood (his wife has no less than three miscarriages while he is researching his biography).

I do not want to give away any of the mysteries that Ms. Vine has so exquisitely contrived, for the joy of this novel is found in her authentic portrayal of the biographer's discoveries. Let's just say that Henry was not a nice man. So much is evident from the start, but precisely how un-nice is what the biographer-hero must determine.

Biography ought to teach us humility. Martin learns as much when he is suddenly presented with a piece of evidence that simply does not fit his developing view of his great-grandfather—or rather, Martin's discovery compels him to re-assess the portrait he has put together in painstaking fashion from diaries, interviews, and extensive reading about his greatgrandfather's research and travels.

Martin learns that Anthony Agnew, the husband of a distant relative, has read a notebook of Henry's that is more revealing than anything Martin has yet seen. Unfortunately, the notebook has been inadvertently thrown into the trash, and Anthony Agnew has suffered a stroke. Will Agnew remember what he read? Even if he does not, though, Agnew's daughter, Caroline, has told Martin that her father felt so sorry for Henry after reading his notebook that he insisted she put flowers on Henry's grave. Evidently, whatever Henry did caused him to experience extraordinary remorse. Martin has already twigged that his illustrious relative committed various crimes, but the biographer is nonplussed by the intense compassion Anthony Agnew feels for Henry, a man Anthony never met or showed any interest in.

In the annals of fiction, Martin Nauther takes his place beside William Dubin, Bernard Malamud's literary biographer-hero in his "Dubin's Lives." Dubin, 60, is writing about D.H. Lawrence's short, passionate life even as he is having an affair with the luscious Fanny, a woman in her early 20s. William could be Martin's American cousin—or rather, the affinity is between Ms. Vine and Mr. Malamud, both of whom show how the complications of the biographer's life inform his choice of subject and help shape the process of research. The result, Ms. Vine and Mr. Malamud show, is a narrative in which the biographer becomes—to adapt a phrase from R.G. Collingwood—his own authority.

Ultimately, Martin is able to plumb the depth of his great-grandfather's great crime not by finding a key document, a key witness, or the proverbial smoking gun, but rather by comparing Anthony Agnew's fragmentary memory of Henry's notebook with what Martin knows about his great-grandfather's reading, his travels, and his profound love for his second son George, a love that seemed entirely out of character.

Toward the end of "The Blood Doctor," passages begin to have a kind of cumulative effect that is reminiscent of the greatest of all novels in this genre, "Absalom, Absalom!" In Faulkner's novel, two college freshmen, Quentin and Shreve, re-interpret the enigmatic life of Thomas Sutpen, a Gothic hero who they bring down to earth, so to speak, during their own intense interaction.

Here is Martin, the biographer, back on the job after being temporarily sidetracked by learning about Anthony Agnew:

But everything that presents itself to me is not like Henry. Confident Henry. Tyrannical Henry. Henry, who deserted one woman after another in order to marry a third he happened to like the look of, and when she died married her sister. Henry, who refused to discuss her brother's [George's] condition with his grown-up daughter and who would have been so adamant in his refusal to let her study medicine that she knew it would be useless to ask him. But, on the other hand, Henry whose wife was the only person who "could do anything with him" and whose son described him as the kindest and sweetest father in the world. Paradoxical Henry.

Henry the enigma.

In such passages, Vine provides a virtual primer on the way a biographer thinks about a "lost world where they order things differently." At times, Martin is an instigator, a liar, and even a cruel cross-examiner. What he finds takes a toll on him and his family just as it did on Henry—but that is another story.

"With all my researches, I know so little of his true nature or his inner life," Martin laments a third of the way through his work on Henry. Yet, in the end, Henry does stand revealed—if not in his innermost being, certainly in the full social, familial, and historical contexts that the best biographies recover.

# Chapter Five

## History and Biography

*William Sloane Coffin: A Holy Impatience* by Warren Goldstein

Biography is not history. Samuel Johnson made this point in The Rambler, No. 60, one of the most important documents in the history of the genre. Biography ought to concern itself not with "vulgar greatness" but with "domestick privacies." He had in mind the kind of detail Boswell later provided about Johnson himself: that he wore a wig too small for his head and hose that drooped around his ankles.

Biographers of public figures have too often shied away from precisely this kind of intimate exposure of their subjects. In the history of our republic, biography refrained (well into this century) from showing our great men in a state of undress. Consciously or unconsciously, American biographers took their cue from their 19th-century forebears: Jared Sparks and his legion, promulgators of historical biography, duly (and dully) concerned only with historical documents and determined to drown any sort of gossip.

To dwell on the private side of a public man's life was deemed a trivialization of history. Besides, it was bad for morale. Biography ought to elevate our public life, provide us with heroes, and spur on our patriotism. All this changed—somewhat—after Lytton Strachey did his demolition job on the high Victorians and biography in Anglo-American literature suddenly opened up to the debunkers. But reviewers still evince distaste for biographers who dig into a public figure's domestic regime, even though—as Johnson noted—what goes on in the tent before the battle (or, I would add, while the microphones are still open) is an aspect of biography as old as Plutarch.

I bring all this background to bear on the biography at hand because I am fascinated with the way Warren Goldstein has handled the personal life of William Sloane Coffin Jr., known by most as the Yale chaplain who counseled young men during the Vietnam War years to resist the draft. Next to Martin Luther King Jr. Mr. Coffin was the most well-known spokesman for liberal Protestantism, his biographer avows. He was a kind of Norman Mailer of the pulpit, a preacher and activist hero.

A World War II veteran and a CIA alumnus, Mr. Coffin was a "man's man," a 20th-century model of the kind of muscular Christianity that had helped to make Britain great in the 19th century. And indeed, in "Armies of the Night" (the title is taken from that magnificent Matthew Arnold poem, "Dover Beach"), Mr. Mailer memorializes the vigorous Mr. Coffin in his entire splendor during the 1968 anti-war march on the Pentagon.

For the first two thirds of this engrossing biography, Mr. Coffin is presented as an admirable hero who nonetheless fails himself at three "moments of truth"—a phrase Mr. Coffin himself favored when he later counseled young men about the draft. Moments one and three have to do with the hero's shying away from combat. Unlike Mr. Mailer, who has described his early self as a "physical coward" but who nevertheless engaged in combat (if only very briefly) in the Pacific, Mr. Coffin was a very physical man who grew up loving a good fistfight, never happier than when he was beating some other man at some form of sport. Coffin served in the U.S. Army in Europe During World War II, but he deliberately avoided combat, preferring to train other soldiers to do the shooting.

The other moment has to do with his realization that he was part of a deal Roosevelt and Stalin struck to repatriate Russian soldiers who had defected to the Germans or for other reasons landed outside the Soviet Union at the end of World War II. The fate for all returnees was the same: execution. Mr. Coffin had to watch as these Russians panicked, attempting suicide in some cases, while they awaited repatriation.

This avoidance of combat and cooperation with evil seems to have influenced Mr. Coffin when he counseled draft resisters. They too faced "a moment of truth," and the chaplain wanted them to realize the full implications of their decision not to go to war. This aspect of Mr. Coffin's biography is compelling and fraught with all kinds of complications, but as I will suggest in due course, Mr. Coffin tended to see the draftees choice from only one perspective: that of the individual's own conscience.

But what of the chaplain's "domestick privacies" during this contentious period of American history? Mr. Goldstein holds backs a good deal until a chapter called "Marriage and Family Life," beginning at page 225. Suddenly we are plunged into the world of Ingmar Bergman. Indeed, the first section of this chapter is titled "Scenes From a Marriage." We learn why Mr. Coffin's first marriage fell apart, and thereafter the domestic front is convulsed in disclosures about his inability to talk to his wives, or share intimate moments with his children, and his comprehensive inability to master everyday tasks.

When Mr. Coffin leaves his second wife, an alcoholic, he does so after he has delivered a late-night judo chop that hospitalizes her. Thereafter, until he meets the woman who becomes his third wife, he is, in the biographer's words, a "mess" who does not even bother to brush his teeth. Admirers of William Sloan Coffin Jr. will wince at the biographer's merciless portrayal, but I hasten to inform them that Mr. Coffin himself was aware of Mr. Goldstein's approach and did nothing to hinder him. Quite the contrary.

Why? Because Mr. Goldstein admires his subject, for all his faults, extravagantly. The biographer's diction is telling: "Coffin had few compunctions about breaking bad laws." If Mr. Coffin had any compunctions, Mr. Goldstein does not say what they were. Mr. Coffin's advocacy of civil disobedience is never seriously challenged in this biography—probably because he did not challenge it himself.

Does a biographer have to challenge his subject? In this case, yes, because Mr. Goldstein seems baffled that Mr. Coffin's brand of liberal Protestantism did not carry the day. After the Vietnam crisis was over, the Evangelicals triumphed, and it does not occur to Mr. Goldstein that there might be a spiritual smugness inherent in the doctrine of civil disobedience that contributed to the demise of liberalism. Evangelicalism, needless to say, is open to the same charge. But that is a column for another day.

How you respond to this biography may depend on whether you are more of an Augustinian (troubled by the sin of desire) or an Aristotelian (beset by the sin of pride).

*Woodrow Wilson* by H. W. Brands
*Woodrow Wilson* by Louis Auchincloss

If you ask a historian to write a biography, you are more likely to get history. Biography puts characters first, while history favors events. Of course, characters and events cannot be easily separated, but one can predominate over the other, depending on the predilections of the narrator. This holds true even when the distinguished historian Arthur M. Schlesinger, Jr.—editor of The American Presidents series, of which this short biography of Woodrow Wilson forms a part—gamely tries to graft biography onto history. In his editor's note, he observes:

Biography offers an easy education in American history, rendering the past more human, more vivid, more intimate, more accessible, more connected to ourselves. Biography reminds us that presidents are not supermen. They are human beings too, worrying about decisions, attending to wives and children, juggling balls in the air, and putting on their pants one leg at a time. Indeed, as Emerson contended, "There is properly no history; only biography."

Quoting Emerson is a scandal—that is, if you are an academic historian. No Ph.D. student would hazard Emersonianisms before a dissertation committee, and beware the untenured professor who would make such an argument for biography. Martin Gilbert, Winston Churchill's authorized biographer, recalls in "In Search of Churchill" that at Oxford his professors never uttered Churchill's name, even though his area of study was appeasement.

In one sense, H.W. Brands is a Schlesingeronian. A historian who holds the Glassock Chair at Texas A&M University, he writes in direct, vivid prose, and he certainly makes the Wilsonian personality accessible—for example, describing the 28th president as the son of a preacher who would justify his political program as the will of God. The historian evinces a biographer's wit when describing President Wilson's effort to oust the Mexican dictator Huerta: "To give God a hand, Wilson stepped up the pressure." When the president's interventionism results in a political mess, Professor Brands describes him as resisting the "temptation to offer Mexico any larger instruction." Thus Mr. Wilson's lofty arrogance is summed up in the kind of deft understatement that a good short biography must employ. Wilson's Mexican disaster is almost comic—and certainly would be so, were Gore Vidal writing this biography.

Professor Brands fulfills the American Presidents series's mission in so far as his book is an economical way of presenting history. It is all there neatly told: Mr. Wilson's family background; his careers as teacher, university president, reform governor of New Jersey, and president; his institution of the income tax; his capitulation to the momentum of war—and then the spectacular defeat of his quest to bring the United States into the League of Nations.

In another sense, however, this book fails as biography. We learn, for example, about Wilson's first wife only as she lies dying. This may have seemed a good move to the historian who wishes to save space for discussion of the policies and events that give Wilson his place in history. Professor Brands does present a tidy passage on the marriage, but segregating Ellen inevitably works against the mission of biography. She never emerges as a person, and it is hard to take her seriously in the paltry paragraph afforded her.

To do partial justice to Ellen, turn to Louis Auchincloss's short biography in the Penguin Lives series: "Ellen was a cultivated and well-educated woman, a talented amateur painter and a poetry lover, with a fine mind that she nonetheless subjugated to her husband's."The truth is—as you'll discover if you read Frances Saunders's biography of Ellen, which neither biographer, alas, includes in his bibliography—Ellen stretched her husband and made him more receptive to others than his aloof sensibility otherwise would permit. If Ellen had survived, perhaps history would not have been different. Perhaps Wilson would still have lost the Senate fight over the treaty determining the structure of the postwar world. But with Ellen alive, at least some of Wilson's actions might have been different. At the very least, his advisors would have had greater access to him.

Wilson, an intolerant man, was not served well by his second wife, Edith. While this much is evident in Professor Brands's description of her actions, the historian does not single out Edith, leaving it to the reader to ferret out how she went about exacerbating her husband's tendency to isolate himself from friends and opponents.

In Mr. Auchincloss's account, Edith appears as nothing less than the villainess, for he begins and ends his biography with excoriating accounts of her meddling efforts to put her husband, rather than the country, first as President Wilson suffered one debilitating stroke after another during the last 17 months of his second term. Edith becomes a character in a Henry James—or even a Louis Auchincloss—novel. Not only did she disserve her country, ultimately she disserved her husband, cutting him off from his closest friends and associates—people like Colonel House, who wrote that his estrangement from President Wilson was a "tragic mystery."

Why did his friend close the door on him? House wondered. "But the key that must unlock the innermost door may still be found," Mr. Auchincloss adds in the concluding sentence of his biography: "It may be discovered in the last word that Woodrow Wilson uttered: "Edith." Perhaps Professor Brands would say Mr. Auchincloss is a little too novelistic in putting so much stress on Edith at the end, but Mr. Auchincloss fulfills biography's mandate: It is a reading of character that rests on that Emersonian aperçu Thomas Hardy rephrased as "Character is fate."

*Stalin: The Court of the Red Tsar* by Simon Sebag Montefiore
*The Unknown Stalin* by Roy and Zhores Medvedev

Historians distrust biography. Modern historiography has rejected Thomas Carlyle's "Great Man" theory of history in favor of complex explorations of historical process, of the forces and factors that shape the world regardless of its individual players. Historians write biography, but they tend to view the genre as a narrative of their subjects' roles in history, not of their subjects' invention of history, so to speak. This determinism is seen as well in late 19th-century naturalism and its offshoots in the 20th century, so that from Thomas Hardy to John Dos Passos, environment—the material conditions of life—tends to prevail over the human spirit.

Marxism contributed to this devaluation of the individual. I remember as an undergraduate reading Trotsky's history of the Russian Revolution, especially his stirring account of Lenin's crucial role. It seemed to me perverse that Trotsky then went on to claim that Lenin himself was not important, that only the historical dynamic expressing itself through Lenin mattered. It seemed to me he had proven that without Lenin, there would not have been a Bolshevik Revolution—or at the very least, that such a revolution would have looked quite different and might even have failed.

Perhaps I was already a budding biographer—taken with Carlyle's argument that,"History is the essence of innumerable biographies." Disraeli puts it more emphatically in his novel,"Contarini Fleming": "Read no history; nothing but biography, for that is life without theory." Emerson went even further: "There is properly no history; only biography." This assertion helps explain why he wrote books like "Representative Men."

I am not such an extremist myself. I rather favor Louis Fischer's formulation: "Biography is history seen through the prism of a person," and something like this is, I take it, the point of "Stalin: The Court of the Red Tsar." Early on, Simon Sebag Montefiore contends:

> Stalin's success was not an accident. No one alive was more suited to the conspiratorial intrigues, theoretical runes, murderous dogmatism and inhuman sternness of Lenin's party. It is hard to find a better synthesis between a man and a movement than the ideal marriage between Stalin and Bolshevism: He was a mirror of its virtues and faults.

Mr. Montefiore's deft combination of biography and history brings Stalin alive, so that he becomes as complex and contradictory as any of the great characters in fiction. Especially riveting is the biographer's account of Stalin's life from 1932 (the year his wife, Nadja, committed suicide) to the eve of World War II. By that point, the Moscow show trials and his war on the peasantry had made Stalin the supreme ruler, a Tsar like Peter the Great, whom the 20th-century dictator greatly admired.

Mr. Montefiore begins with a great set piece—the day of Nadja's sudden death, an event so abrupt and shocking that rumors quickly spread alleging Stalin had murdered her. The biographer discounts the possibility of foul play, but he uses this profoundly troubling incident to introduce the court of powerful party leaders (he calls them magnates) that supported Stalin, and he shows how Stalin's reaction to the suicide became a turning point in his life and in the history of the

Soviet Union. Indeed, as more than one of the biographer's sources insists, thereafter Stalin was a different man.

After Nadja died, Stalin no longer danced—or so he said, perhaps to emphasize that his ability to take pleasure outside the world of politics had diminished. He felt his wife had punished him by taking her life. He called himself a broken man. He never stopped trying to understand why she committed suicide—sometimes admitting that he had failed her as a husband, and sometimes accusing her of abandoning him.

Mr. Montefiore dispels the notion that Stalin drove his wife to her death, but it was a stormy marriage filled with many quarrels. Nadja frequently disagreed with her husband's policies or with his treatment of people. Her own family, however, regarded her as unbalanced and often sympathized with Stalin. She herself was a committed Marxist and proud of her husband; she, like the rest of the members in the court around Stalin, never doubted his greatness or his fitness to rule. Indeed, Stalin expected his courtiers to sacrifice themselves for him, which they did not merely because he was a fearful tyrant but because they shared his fanatical commitment to Marxism-Leninism. Certainly men like Beria and Khrushchev were careerists and used the Party to get ahead, but ideology—the idea of building a better world and tearing down the bad old capitalist one—fueled the myth built around a cult of personality, the "man of steel."

In other words, Stalin was as necessary to his court as to himself. He was not merely some cunning monster who hijacked Lenin's role in the Revolution. His very brutality proved his seriousness, his commitment to the cause, his willingness to do anything to ensure the Communist Revolution prevailed. Killing millions made him an awe-inspiring figure among his courtiers, who themselves traveled the Soviet Union on what can only be termed killing tours.

But the mass-murdering Stalin, the Stalin of the purge trials, in which a whole generation of old Bolsheviks and army officers lost their lives, is largely the product of that man who emerged after 1932. Before then, especially between 1925 and 1932, Stalin was consolidating his power, expelling Trotsky, but also charming his rivals and critics.

Stalin was a voracious reader and had an aesthetic sense, though he was willing to distort it in the interests of Party hegemony. He loved Dostoevsky but did not want him taught to the young because the author might demoralize them. Always a good politician, Stalin lured Gorky back to the Soviet Union and made him a Party propagandist. And Stalin befriended other writers who supported his grandiose five-year plans to reconstruct the country as an industrial and cultural power.

Stalin accomplished a great deal without using terror, yet his resort to torture and murder after 1932—after Nadja's death—became central to his government.

Mr. Montefiore does not say in so many words why Stalin changed. But from the narrative it is clear that Stalin closed up emotionally. His wife's death hurt him too much. She had made him vulnerable. His grief was a matter of public record. He broke down several times, cried, and for a short period seemed incapable of ruling. And then, as he recovered, he ruled, as they say, with a vengeance.

Mr. Montefiore, like Disraeli, does not present theories, but his narrative reveals why Stalin changed. Stalin could never accept that someone so close to him could, in his view, betray him. If Nadja could kill herself and leave an accusatory note behind, then who was not (potentially) a traitor to Stalin? Who was not a traitor—in theory, if not in fact? Who would not betray him later, if not sooner? The idea of betrayal infected Stalin; it became his chronic disease. This was also the chronic disease of his party, since Bolshevism prided itself on purity of motivations and the Bolsheviks—like the Puritans—could never be certain that the congregation's purity would be preserved.

The Bolsheviks saw themselves as surrounded by a corrupt world. They themselves were part of it, saved only because of their conversion experience. But these were men—and a few women like Nadja—who had been brought up as Christians. They even continued to sing the hymns of their childhood at Bolshevik parties. Stalin, an ex-choir boy, and his ex-Christian cohort were grounded in the story of a savior and his Judas. And who was Judas? A disciple. Stalin was always suspicious of the men who wanted to be close to Stalin.

To his credit, Mr. Montefiore does not press such a theory. He narrates. He makes his point by putting Nadja's story first—not Stalin's childhood, not his early career, but the suicide that was a cataclysmic dividing point in the biography of an individual and in the history of a nation.

Next to Mr. Montefiore almost any other writing about Stalin—Solzhenitsyn excepted—will probably pale. "The Unknown Stalin" has none of Mr. Montefiore's flair. Indeed, although the publishers call it a biography, it is no such thing. It is rather chapters or essays about aspects of Stalin's life and career. As a reference work, it is up to date and comes with the authority of authors who are scholars and participants in Soviet history.

The Medvedevs do try to create some suspense: "Was there a plot to murder Stalin?" they ask in the first chapter. The second sentence should contain the answer, which is no, but of course such a revelation might deter further reading, and that would be a shame, since the Medvedevs do clarify a good many historiographical and biographical issues.

For example, in a chapter on the atomic bomb, they lay out what Soviet scientists knew about atomic energy and the role that Klaus Fuchs played in making the Soviet bomb a virtual copy of the American one. (The Rosenbergs, by the way, are not even mentioned as a factor.) Other important issues, such as the

Nazi-Soviet pact and whether with a little luck Hitler could have in blitzkrieg fashion defeated the Soviet Union, are canvassed with thoroughness and good sense.

"The Unknown Stalin" sports a blurb from Mr. Montefiore, which is welcome confirmation of my conclusion that these two books complement and strengthen each other.

## *An Unfinished Life: John F. Kennedy, 1917–1963* by Robert Dallek

Can biography ever be definitive? Publishers pretend it can be so. "Now at long last," Robert Dallek's publisher proclaims, "we have the definitive biography of Jack Kennedy."

A publisher's hyperbole is not ordinarily worthy of comment, but reviewers, too, have hailed this account as conclusive and authoritative. Typical of the cheerleading is Ted Widmer in the New York Times Book Review: "Thanks to Dallek's findings, things make sense at an entirely new level." Referring to the biographer's handling of JFK's medical problems, Mr. Widmer exclaims, "Suddenly, the most famous celebrity in modern American history is something more vulnerable—a living organism, fighting for survival from the day he was born."

Forgotten is Nigel Hamilton's "JFK: Reckless Youth" (1992), which did a splendid job of revealing that Kennedy's dire ill health began to manifest itself in his childhood and teenage years. Mr. Hamilton explored the diagnosis of Addison's disease and the complications from venereal disease that had JFK battling urinary tract infections for most of his life. Only one writer in my Lexis-Nexis survey of more than 40 reviews even mentions Mr. Hamilton's groundbreaking biography. What does Mr. Dallek present that is not available in previous biographies? The JFK presidential library granted him access to medical records that reveal a more complete and dramatic record of the most overmedicated president in American history. This is valuable material that Mr. Dallek skillfully integrates into his narrative, but neither these additional details nor his handling of other aspects of President Kennedy's life constitute anything approaching the term "definitive." That Mr. Dallek alone among the numerous Kennedy scholars was granted access to these files raises questions about the kind of biography—if indeed it is a biography—reviewers have extolled.

Actually, Mr. Dallek does not claim to be definitive. In his extensive notes and acknowledgments, he gives full credit to books and articles that are the "indispensable starting point for a biographer." His aim, however, is to make his book the standard one-volume authority on JFK: "My objective has not been to write another debunking book (these have been in ample supply in recent years) but to penetrate the veneer of glamour and charm to reconstruct the real man or as close to it as possible." Note that Mr. Dallek does not attack the debunkers. How could he, when his notes section repeatedly cites their work? Ever the gentleman scholar, he uses words like "judicious" and "balanced" in describing his approach. Balance, however, like beauty, is apparently in the eye of the beholder.

Certainly Mr. Hamilton did not think of himself as injudicious or unbalanced. He set out to write "a complete life in the English tradition," he pointed out in his author's note and acknowledgments. His aim was to create a "serious, balanced, and scholarly biography." Yet Mr. Hamilton abandoned his three-volume life after encountering opposition from the Kennedy family and impediments put in his way by the "exquisitely located John F. Kennedy Library at Columbia Point, overlooking Boston Harbor," as the more fortunate Mr. Dallek describes the repository in his acknowledgments.

Why did Mr. Dallek find favor while Mr. Hamilton, the author of a threevolume authorized life of Field Marshall Montgomery, was turned away? Mr. Dallek, author of an acclaimed two-volume biography of Lyndon Johnson, notes, among other reasons for his access, his reputation for evenhandedness. What does this mean? It means that for every negative, he finds a positive. In Mr. Hamilton's book, JFK's father appears as a rather scurrilous character. A stock manipulator of genius and a world-class lecher, Joseph Kennedy was also a political schemer who, as a U.S. ambassador to Britain, became in effect a Neville Chamberlain advisor and a subverter of his own president's policies. In Mr. Dallek's narrative, Joe is an admired athlete, an adored elder brother with an "infectious grin," a "brilliant banker," and "keen observer" of "contemporary American financial practices." In other words, Joe's juicy life is sucked dry by prose that eliminates him as a living character. Here is how Mr. Dallek treats Joseph Kennedy's repeated adulteries: "Joe's independence and willingness to defy accepted standards partly expressed itself in compulsive womanizing." It is hardly womanizing at all when put into Mr. Dallek's pacifying prose.

Mr. Hamilton crafted a biography that reads like an 18th-century picaresque novel. His structure is episodic with inviting chapter subtitles like "a very lively elf" (describing the young JFK) and "weaving daydreams" (evoking early signs of the famous JFK wit). Mr. Dallek, in contrast, is all business with sober chapter titles like "The Congressman" and "The Senator." Indeed, Mr. Dallek's chapter titles reveal that he is writing not a full-scale biography, but a political or intellectual biography with some personal matters thrown in. Jackie Kennedy hardly makes an appearance in this long book.

It needs to be said that starting with Plutarch, biography takes the measure of the whole man. Plutarch thought it important to note that Coriolanus was a mama's boy. Mr. Dallek seems to understand the meaning of biography, but he is so keen to get on with accounts of the Cuban Missile Crisis and other world-shaking events that time and again he shows no curiosity in precisely what he claims at the outset as his interest: to know "the real man." The "real man" is absent, for example, in Mr. Dallek's discussion of "Profiles in Courage." The book was JFK's idea, but its series of narratives was essentially written by a committee of friends and associates, and then reshaped by Kennedy, who served more as editor than author. When the book won a Pulitzer Prize, Mr. Dallek notes, this event "sparked predictable envy" and generated charges that Kennedy had not written the work that bore his name. It is hard to see balance at work here when the biographer limits his criticism to noting a single motivation after presenting evidence amounting to an indictment of Kennedy's actions just a few pages earlier in the narrative.

Similarly, after detailing JFK's complex medical history (which would have disqualified him from seeking the presidency if the public had known about it), Mr. Dallek quotes JFK: "I'm forty-three years old, and I'm the healthiest candidate for President in the United States." Was Mr. Kennedy joking? Mr. Dallek makes much of JFK's "realism," his willingness to face facts, and to live without illusions. But JFK's own words seem to pass by the biographer who in the sentence following JFK's boast simply refers to his subject's confidence. To be fair, Mr. Dallek later remarks that JFK "enjoyed" overcoming his illnesses. In this instance, he finds just the right word to capture his subject's spirited personality, which provided such a vivid contrast with the grim determination of rivals like Richard Nixon.

So many opportunities pass Mr. Dallek by. When JFK meets George Wallace, the latter engages in a tirade against Martin Luther King Jr., accusing him of womanizing. All Mr. Dallek reports about this exchange is that JFK was "not amused." This meeting is recounted in a Pierre Salinger memo given to the biographer by Sheldon Stern, Mr. Dallek is careful to explain in the notes. But what did JFK say? To focus on this instance is to reveal an alarming void in this biography: Where are the interviews? Mr. Dallek mentions speaking to several individuals, but few of them are identified in his acknowledgments, and his notes contain only scattered references to interviews. This unfinished biography is rather like what R.G. Collingwood calls "scissors and paste history," a patching together of documents. The patchwork accounts, in part, for the rather leaden feel of this biography.

Almost all of Mr. Dallek's details about JFK's sex life come from Seymour Hersh's "The Dark Side of Camelot" (1997), one of those debunking biographies. Although Mr. Dallek mentions JFK's meetings with Marilyn Monroe, he does so in such a muted fashion that it is not clear where to place Monroe in order of importance in the president's sex life. Does this omission matter? Not to readers who want a précis of the public man, the politician and statesman, but to those who wanted to see the "real man," it matters a good deal. The biographer's bibliography does not list any of the significant biographies of Monroe by Anthony Summers, Donald Spoto, and Barbara Leaming—all of whom render verdicts on the importance of MM in JFK's life.

Also missing from Mr. Dallek's acknowledgments is the kind of engagement with his subject that Mr. Hamilton demonstrated when he remarked, "In undertaking this biography, I called upon many distinguished authors and historians who toiled in the field of JFK studies before me." It is this inquiring dialogue with sources—which requires getting up from the library seat and going out on a chase after living history—that Mr. Dallek's work lacks. Blessed with his own wealth of archival material, Mr. Hamilton nevertheless conducted "fresh interviews with surviving JFK friends and historical witnesses" who "enabled me to round out and balance the vast JFK Library oral history program." The result is a biography that moves at a smart pace even though it is 800 pages long and ends with JFK's first congressional campaign.

To all this Robert Dallek might respond: "But you are demanding a book I did not intend to write." Precisely so. Will Nigel Hamilton please resume his work?

# Chapter Six

## *Literary Biography*

*Erich Maria Remarque: The Last Romantic* by Hilton Tims

How literary does a literary biography have to be? Biographer Justin Kaplan believes the literary biographer should aspire to write in a style that turns biography into an aesthetic object. This is what reviewers seem to be lauding when they claim that certain biographies read like novels. But how to attain that art and at the same time do justice to the literary subject's work? Literary criticism is the nemesis of narrative, the cross on which so many literary biographies come to grief. Analysis anesthetizes the story; interpretation distances the reader from the flow of events; plot summaries become roadblocks on the biographer's route to the evocation of a life.

Hilton Tims, a British journalist, novelist, and critic, surmounts these difficulties by selecting telling details, deftly providing one-paragraph synopses of novels, quoting distinctive passages, and then placing the work in the context of the night of May 10, 1933, when the Nazis staged a public burning of Remarque's famous pacifist novel, "All Quiet on the Western Front".

This is a story worth knowing, since Mr. Remarque would also be branded a pacifist for the rest of his life. This is all accomplished in a few pages, resulting in a streamlined, sensible, and often elegant book—a state-of-theart specimen of literary biography.

Mr. Remarque was obliged to flee Germany when the Nazis took power, and Germany never forgave him for writing novels about the Holocaust from the safety (so his countrymen believed) of exile. Mr. Tims's subject, Erich Maria Remarque, is still best known for his anti-war novel, "All Quiet on the Western

Front" (1929), a sensitive and passionate work that led the Nazis to behead his own sister for sharing her brother's "defeatist" views.

But the novelist was no pacifist, Mr. Tims explains. Indeed, not only did Remarque see action in World War I, he was also wounded—and, rather like Ernest Hemingway, later dramatized and expanded on his own brush with death. Remarque supported the fight against fascism in World War II. But to communists, to Nazis, to almost any fervent political ideologue or nationalist, the novelist remained an example of the defeatist mentality that made him feel like an exile all his life—no matter where he resided—be it New York, Hollywood, or his beloved Casa Remarque in Switzerland.

The biographer calls his subject "The Last Romantic" because Remarque remained a sensitive outcast, unable to commit himself fully to any culture outside of Germany and unable to feel he could ever return to live in his native land. Love—the pursuit of beautiful, famous, and bossy women like Marlene Dietrich, Greta Garbo, and Paulette Goddard—became his method of inventing his own world. These strong women found the unpretentious but courtly Mr. Remarque irresistible, even though he was not a high-powered lover (indeed, his diaries note instances of impotence). But these women empathized with of the horror of war as it impinges on Paul Baumer, a teenage recruit in "All Quiet on the Western Front". An international bestseller, the novel became controversial in Germany because unlike so many of his countrymen Mr. Remarque did not attempt to justify his nation's participation in World War I or to mitigate its sense of humiliating defeat. (The fine film adaptation of the novel made the young Lew Ayres not only a star but also a lifelong pacifist. The actor, Mr. Tims reminds us, jeopardized his career by refusing to fight in World War II, even though he came under fire as a paramedic.) It is altogether fitting, then, that the biographer focuses on Remarque's passive-aggressive qualities that kept the game of love going. Here is Mr. Tims's adroit handling of the complicated Ms. Dietrich:

> Marlene's dalliance with Joe Carstairs [a lesbian] became a torment. Almost certainly there was an element of manipulation behind it, her fickle moods testing him [Remarque], provoking his jealousy, creating situations she could resolve with some generous or affectionate gesture or a brief resumption of intimacy. And Remarque at his lowest emotional ebb was a pitifully easy target for her capriciousness.
> His diary entries are a jagged graph of his feelings…The musical chairs of comings and goings, finding Marlene's door locked against him and knowing Joe is behind it with her…the intensities seething below the surface of all these relationships would take on a quality of farce were it not for the anguish Remarque was genuinely suffering.

The biographer never assumes too much—note his "almost certainly." He employs his novelist's sense of immediacy by shifting to the present tense: "Joe is behind it with her."

This excellent biography includes only one disappointment. Where is the summing up? It is one thing not to burden the narrative with literary criticism; it is another to leave the reader wondering how good a writer the biographer believes his subject to be. Mr. Tims quotes reviews but only occasionally ventures an opinion himself. This biography ends with an epilogue, a good place to learn which of Mr. Remarque's novels still matter, but the biographer remains mute on that subject, which seems strange behavior for a novelist and critic.

*A Tragic Honesty: The Life and Work of Richard Yates* by Blake Bailey

Who first propounded the preposterous notion that writers' lives do not make for good biography? Supposedly nothing significant happens in a writer's life except for the writing. Most writers are not men or women of action. E.L. Doctorow once told me in an interview that his biography would make dull reading. That is like saying the life of the imagination has no story to tell. Or was it just the writer's way of warding off a prospective biographer? Writers—even autobiographical novelists like Richard Yates—have a horror of the naked narrative and are shocked when one of their fellows forsakes fiction for the starker precincts of memoir as William Stryon did with "Darkness Visible," an account of his suicidal depression. Even though Yates put himself, his family, and writer-friends like Styron into his novels, he was appalled when Styron denuded himself in nonfiction.

Biography strips bare—that is why novelists like Joyce Carol Oates detest what she calls "pathography," a term she coined when reviewing a biography of Jean Stafford that faithfully reported the prolonged mental and physical debilitation that made writing virtually impossible in Stafford's later years. The biography was true to the arc of Stafford's life but not to the importance of her writing. When a subsequent biography focused on Stafford's writing and downplayed her foibles, critics applauded.

Such hostility to biography—especially among the literati and the academic community—requires rectification. "It is frequently objected to relations of particular lives that they are not distinguished by any striking or wonderful vicissitudes," Samuel Johnson wrote. This desire for dramatic doings is prompted, he argued, by "false measures of excellence and dignity." Biographers should eradicate such prejudices by passing "slightly over those performances and incidents, which produced vulgar greatness, to lead the thoughts into domestick privacies, and display the minute details of daily life, where exterior appendages are cast aside, and men excel each other only by prudence and by virtue." Johnson was not speaking only for himself; he relied on no less of an authority than Montaigne, who confessed: "I have a singular curiosity to pry into the souls and the natural and true opinions of the authors with whom I converse." He would much rather learn about what Brutus said in his tent the night before a battle than about the speech the hero delivered the next day for public consumption.

Fortunately, Blake Bailey does not spare us Richard Yates's agonies—his lifelong alcoholism, psychotic episodes, failed marriages, and doubts about the value of his writing—any more than Yates spared his characters their indignities. April and Frank Wheeler, the principal figures in his greatest novel, "Revolutionary Road" (1961), begin their marriage in a 1950s Connecticut suburb—terrain familiar to readers of John Updike and John Cheever, to whom Yates has often been compared—with a sense of superiority, a dream of greatness that they manifestly will not be able to fulfill. It is an old story, the gap between aspiration and achievement, but Yates redeems the cliché by the vividness of his observations and his unrelenting, unsentimental revelation that this couple is not much different from their mediocre neighbors. This Gatsbyesque fable of thwarted dreams would become Yates's signature tale, told again and again in exquisitely wrought stories and novels that critics praised for their art and condemned for their pessimism. As a result he failed to capture the larger audience that gravitated toward Cheever and Updike. Yates might have been in the running for awards, but he was always the kind of writer who just missed the prize.

Let us hope Mr. Bailey will be the one finally to thrust Yates into the literary canon. He has written not merely a splendid biography of Yates—one that makes a compelling case for his subject's greatness and explains why he has been neglected—but one of the most moving and engrossing literary biographies of our times. Mr. Bailey seductively interweaves the facts and fiction of Yates's life into a fine mesh of life and literature, which, the biographer candidly notes, cannot always be disentangled. First drafts of Yates's work used real names, and even the final drafts made only superficial changes, so that, for example, his mother's nickname, Dookie, becomes Pookie. Mark Twain once said that history did not repeat itself, it rhymed. That is how Yates used fiction—as a kind of rhyme for his life.

There is wonderful comedy in Yates's self-destructiveness just as there is in the lives of his self-destructive characters. Bailey knows how to present it:

> He wanted to be a proper country husband, a productive member of his household and community. He wanted to show he could "pull his weight," "stay on the ball," and "cope" as well or better than the most banal bore in Redding, but his efforts had a way of ending badly. One morning while his wife was fixing breakfast he went outside to burn

some trash. A few minutes later he let loose an aria of obscenities, but the jaded Sheila [his first wife] simply assumed he'd stubbed his toe and went on with her business. Finally, she glanced outside: there was a brushfire in the backyard, on the edges of which Yates gamboled ineffectually. The volunteer fire department arrived in time to save their house, and a penitent Yates agreed to become a member, faithfully attending meetings every Saturday night.

Literary life is often portrayed as a competitive free-for-all; it may be that, but it can also be a heroic world in which writers like R.V. Cassill, Grace Schulman, and George Garrett treat Yates with an uplifting generosity and respect. Biography may strip its subjects bare, but in this case it also brilliantly restores the life and work of a great artist.

# Chapter Seven

# Brief Biographies

*Robert E. Lee* by Roy Blount, Jr.

Brief biographies have so many pleasures and advantages that it is rather surprising that before James Atlas no one thought to propose the Penguin Lives series, to which Roy Blount, Jr.'s splendid "Robert E. Lee" has just been added. Decades ago Leon Edel admonished contemporary biographers for including too much of the mountainous modern archives in their congested narratives. Biographers like Matthew Bruccoli did not heed the warning. When asked why one would write another biography of Scott Fitzgerald, he replied, "more facts."

Sometimes less is more. That Lee, for example, liked his children to tickle his toes assumes a greater importance in a 200-page biography than it would in Douglas Southall Freeman's four-volume version. Mr. Blount, by the way, refers to Mr. Freeman as Lee's "doting biographer" and quotes a passage from Mr. Freeman that suggests why the long biography can go awry while the short one can seem so apposite: Freeman insists, "there is no inconsistency to be explained, no enigma to be solved" in Lee, whose character's "essential elements…were two and only two, simplicity and spirituality." In principle that is true of, say, water, but go find a river that pure. Mr. Blount agrees that Lee was pure—a man of unquestioned integrity, a religious man, a gentleman—but not that pure, since he chose to defend the South and its institution of slavery even though his step-grandfather, George Washington, clearly named it an evil that should be eradicated sooner rather than later. At Gettysburg, Lee led his men into a slaughter that at least one of his distinguished subordinates (Longstreet) opposed. Lee committed that blunder, General Grant speculated, because his "blood was up." Right or wrong, Grant and Mr. Blount both see Lee as an enigma who had rash as well as restrained traits that have never been satisfactorily explained.

One of the delights of Mr. Blount's biography is that his witty comment on Mr. Freeman occurs in the bibliography. In other words, every part of this "short snort," as one of my favorite history professors used to call such books, is entertaining and incisive. Mr. Blount fulfills Mr. Atlas's keen desire first to find good writers and then match them to the right subject (in this case a writer with Southern roots and an irreverent sense of humor).

Like some others in the Penguin Lives series, Mr. Blount has not distinguished himself in biography heretofore. It is unlikely that at the start he was all that familiar with the primary source material. But the biographer in brief often relies on the best secondary sources—in this case on what Mr. Blount calls Emory Thomas's "definitive biography," "Robert E. Lee" (1995): "Thomas is considerably and considerately shorter-winded than Freeman, and a master of chapterization: the beginnings, endings, and titles of his chapters are inspired." Note again, it is the writing, not just the research that counts.

In a sense, the short biography can extend our notion of biography more than the long one does. Biographers in brief often comment in the narrative itself on previous biographers, whereas their more wordy counterparts too often ignore the competition, except in their end matter. Mr. Blount challenges us to think again about a familiar figure that has been refracted through generations of biographical narratives. The short biography can become a work of historiography. Mr. Blount's publisher also presents us with an astounding claim: This is the "first brief biography of this American legend." Even if that claim—how brief is brief?—might just be a bit of a stretcher, there are apparently no serious contenders.

In the narrative proper, Mr. Blount presents a fairly straightforward account of Lee's life and career, emphasizing nonetheless his desire to please his mother, to compensate for his father's ("Light Horse Harry" Lee) reckless behavior, and to remain true to his native state no matter his qualms about slavery.

The most remarkable aspect of Mr. Blount's biography are his three appendices, in which he gives freer reign to psychological speculation and attempts to draw parallels with contemporary life. Thus we are treated to sentences that join together Elvis and Robert as Southern boys and mamma's boys, and to William Faulkner's evocation in "Intruder in the Dust" of what it means to be a Southern boy. It does not go unnoticed that Lee had small feet and that other parts of his body had an erotic attraction for both men and women. The "marble man"—as Lee was often called—is shown in another appendix to have had a sense of humor. Finally, his views on slavery are put in context with those of his contemporaries and predecessors.

Mr. Blount's tendency to use analogies may disturb historicist readers—that is, those who insist on viewing Lee as a man of his time whose actions must be explained in the context of his epoch. Mr. Blount suggests that Lee was "personally against slavery the way a Nike executive might personally be against Indonesian sweatshops if he had to feed, clothe, and house the workers and live surrounded by them—Isn't there some way we can do without these people?" But in the next sentence Mr. Blount does return to history: "Like Lincoln, Lee was favorably disposed toward the relocation of freedmen to Africa, and he may in fact have transported to Liberia some slaves he had no use for."

On the biggest question of all, Mr. Blount can do no better than to quote Emory Thomas, showing in the process how biography and history intersect:

Had Lee chosen to remain in the United States Army or had he resigned and only raised corn while men fought and died, he would have elected infamy. He would have had to spend the rest of his life explaining his actions to deaf ears. And not the least of a legion of accusers would have been his own wife, who became a fiercely partisan Confederate. Robert Lee would have been most in danger in his own bed. In a real sense, Lee went to war in order to avoid conflict.

*Marcel Proust* by Mary Ann Caws

The Overlook Press has revived an old genre: the short pictorial biography. Each volume in the series contains over a hundred photographs and illustrations. Mary Ann Caws, who has already published a well-received Overlook life of Virginia Woolf, demonstrates in the first Proustian sentence of her "Prelude" the symbiosis between words and pictures, and between biographer and subject:

> If the great book about the quest of time still holds such magnetism now, it passes by way of the caricatures of Proust in bed, Proust and his Madeleine, Proust and his heavy overcoat—sometimes fur on the outside, sometimes inside—the coat with a velvet color, that collar always reaching his drooping dark mustache under his melancholy dark-ringed eyes.

These images, she is right to say, dominate and shape contemporary literary consciousness even if one has not read Proust—or, like me—can claim to have read only parts of the master. Proust has become a synecdoche of the consciousness that savors the past like a Madeleine (now available at Starbucks), the cynosure of the effete aesthete who made a kind of heroic gesture out of perception, enforcing the idea that to observe, however preciously, is to participate in the creation of the world. He forms part of the visual inventory of great writers we fashion in our mind's eye. We transport his visage on tote bags; we drink out of his mug. If we know a bit of Proust biography, we understand that that heavy overcoat represents the Proust who was always cold, who wanted the room temperature to be 86 degrees, the invalid writer who was never more engaged with the world than when he retreated to his corklined room to shut out the distracting noise of that world, which competed with his own complete vision of it. As Ms. Caws concludes, "Proust's marveling at the world and his withdrawal from it are, in a sense, of a piece."

More than any other writer I can think of, Proust seems like a character in someone else's novel—like someone else's invention, in other words, of a great writer consumed by his work. That Proust, I venture to say, is the creation of George Painter, Proust's first great biographer in English. Mr. Painter's ambition was appropriately Proustian: "I have endeavored to write a definitive biography of Proust: a complete, exact and detailed narrative of his life, that is, based on every known or discoverable primary source, and on primary sources only," he wrote in the first volume of his audacious biography (two volumes, 1959 and 1965—a revised version in a single volume was published in 1989).

Mr. Painter saw himself as rescuing Proust from the Proustians, those academics and adepts who called "À la Recherche du Temps Perdu" a "closed system, containing in itself all the elements necessary for its understanding." The biographer pointed out that in fact Proust could not be vacuum-packed. No critic could discuss a work of literature without, consciously or unconsciously, applying what he knew about the author and his period. Mr. Painter, casting himself in heroic mode, set out to crush the Proust industry:

> The "closed system" Proustians have been egoistically contented to know of Proust's novel only what it means to themselves. It is surely relevant to learn what the novel meant to the author, to understand the special significance which, because they were part of his life and being, every character and episode had for Proust and still retains in its substance. What do they know of "À la Recherche du Temps Perdu" who only "À la Recherche" know?

Quoting Keats, Mr. Painter argued that the novel was an allegory of Proust's life: "A man's life of any worth is a continual allegory." And it is the symbolic power of Mr. Painter's writing that ensures his work will not date any more than Boswell's does. In Painter, Proust is the embodiment of the 20$^{th}$-century writer.

Which returns us to the biography at hand. Ms. Caws's evocation of the way we visualize Proust makes her biography stand apart from the insuperable writer who was George Painter, and more recently…those of Ronald Hayman, William Sansom, the brief and convincing one by Edmund White, the massive and authoritative work of William Carter and the classically French approach of Jean-Yves Tadié. Another "massive tome," she suggests, is not needed—and neither is another short conventional one, I would add. Instead, her biography's dialogue between pictures and text becomes an extension of what we already know. Thus she begins a sentence in her second chapter, "Guiding Threads," sounding as if she is agreeing with some other biography of Proust we have just read: "Yes, his mother hovered over him ceaselessly, as his letters to her do over her."

Most biographies contain pictures, but in Ms. Caws's book, you cannot turn a page without confronting a picture. Most biographies have one or two portraits of important figures. Ms. Caws has no less than four of Count Robert de Montesquiou-Fezenzac (1855–1921), showing the model for the Baron de Charlus, Proust's most memorable character, in several of his flamboyant guises. The biographer augments these illustrations with powerful word-pictures of her own, describing Charlus's real-life model: "With his rouged cheeks, his wavy thick black hair and mustache and his tiny teeth no less black, that he would hide behind a dainty hand when he laughed, with his pink Liberty cravat and his green waistcoat."

The biographer's own style resembles a snapshot: "I have chosen a nonlinear approach, with the various directions taken in as free a manner as the novel itself and the life of reading it leads to." Thus there are chapters on Proust's reading, how he appeared to observers like Colette, what his daily life was like, the women and men who fascinated him, what Proust liked to look at and listen to. Such an approach is quite satisfying for a reader who already knows a bit of Proust and would like to dwell on the harmonies of Ms. Caws's prose and pictures. Perhaps a raw beginner ought to tackle Mr. White's Penguin Life first, then Ms. Caws, then Mr. Painter, before taking on behemoths like Tadié or Carter.

Ms. Caws pays Mr. Painter no mind, but most biographers cannot resist jousting with him because of the polemical preface to his biography. Edmund White noted that Mr. Painter took the funniest bits from the memoirs of Proust's period but did not interview any of his friends or acquaintances. It would seem an odd bit of behavior in a biographer who aimed to be definitive. But I think I know why. I once heard a biographer of Marianne Moore respond to a question about whom he had spoken with in the course of his research. "Oh, interviews are so messy," he replied. It is not that Mr. Painter accepted written words as more trustworthy than oral testimony (why should one be more accurate than the other?), but to sit through an interview (as any biographer can tell you) is to submit yourself to someone else's authority. Conversation is an unstable text, and the biographer must choose what to use out of all the gabble. Writing imposes coherence, even if it is sometimes a factitious one.

Jean-Yves Tadié, a formidable authority on Proust, pummeled Mr. Painter for the lack of interviews: "There were some people who did not write anything, and others who did not write down all they knew. All that is irretrievably lost." And apparently Mr. Painter is to blame. "It was a world André Maurois knew well. His well-balanced biography has been forgotten, because he did not pride himself on a cheap knowledge of Freud," M. Tadié complained. Even Mr. Painter's greatest achievement gets a Gallic going over: "Painter's success, as Barthes has shown, lies mainly in this impression it gives of reading a novel, one that is both about a life and a work, avoiding the immense effort required to read 'À la Recherche du Temps Perdu.'"

M. Tadié's alternative, however, has its own hazards, according to Mr. White: "When I first skimmed the 952-page text I seriously underestimated its worth, since it lacks narrative sweep and humor value and sometimes looks just like random notes." But on a more careful reading Mr. White discovered a "masterpiece," devoid of critical cant and informed by a study of Proust's manuscripts with "more thoroughness and understanding than anyone else alive."

Skulking within M. Tadié's tirade against Mr. Painter is the accusation often leveled at literary biography: that it absolves the reader from actually confronting the writer's work. The biographer digests the literature for you, and there we are again at the Barnes & Noble or Border's café, making a meal of writers' lives. M. Tadié and his type may have a point, but it is just a point, for it can be argued, conversely, that biography stimulates the appetite for literature—or if that is too bold a claim, substitute the word "sustains."

The first picture in Ms. Caws's "Prelude" is (the caption reads) "Proust in overcoat, from Stephanie Huet, the Proust Comic Book." Ms. Caws knows that it is not a bad thing to perpetuate Proust in every way we can with whatever aid to digestion we require.

## *Carl Sandburg: Adventures of a Poet* by Penelope Niven

Some of the best brief biographies are written for children. A case in point is Penelope Niven's "Carl Sandburg: Adventures of a Poet." Like many other biographies for children, it is exquisitely illustrated (in this instance by Marc Nadel), and it presents both a chronological and thematic view of its subject. The first chapter, "A World of Words," situates Carl Sandburg in his milieu and in his art:

> Carl August Sandburg was born on a corn-husk mattress in a three-room house in Galesburg, Illinois, soon after midnight on January 6, 1878. The first words drifting into his ears were "Det är en pojke!" Swedish for "It is a boy!" Carl was the first son of Clara and August Sandburg, who had left their homes in Sweden as young adults to start new lives in the United States. Carl grew up loving words...

Ms. Niven, the author of a full-length biography, "Carl Sandburg: A Biography" (1991), has written a beginning chapter for children that is far more compelling than the first paragraphs she wrote for adults. But this observation is actually beside the point: Children's biographies are not just for children! What is childish, or childlike, about what I have quoted? Writing for children should be every bit as good as writing for adults; the reader ought to be plunged into the story of a life through the use of vivid images, sounds, and stark facts.

This particular biography has another compelling aspect: no photographs. Instead, Mr. Nadel, an award-winning illustrator, serves virtually as a co-author, creating, for example, a title spread that pictures Carl Sandburg walking past a warehouse in the turn-of-the-century Chicago he wrote about so boldly and pictorially. The spread is a sort of mural, just as the building itself is a mural of the objects that defined Sandburg's life: the milk bottles he delivered as a "milk slinger"; his soldier's hat and Spanish American War medal; his guitar; a train of the type he hopped as a hobo; the cover of his children's book, "Rootabaga Stories"; and a reproduction of "Fog," his most famous poem, in his own handwriting.

This is biography of a high order, biography as an aesthetic object. I cannot think of a better way to introduce anyone to all that biography has to offer than to point out the fine interplay not only between Ms. Niven's words and Mr. Nadel's pictures but between their evocation of Sandburg and the book's reproduction of his writings—which are themselves bordered by Mr. Nadel's illustrations. So-called children's biographies often achieve a richness and unity of effect that are rarely equaled in biographies for adults.

Reading children's biographies also serves as an antidote to the cant one finds every week in book reviews. I'm thinking of those reviewers who are hostile to literary biography, who tiresomely repeat the notion that it is the work that counts, not the artist's life. Tell that to any child who wants to know about his favorite author. As Samuel Johnson remarked in his "Life of Savage": "The heroes of literary as well as civil history have been very often no less remarkable for what they have suffered than for what they have achieved."

Ms. Niven relates in "Carl Sandburg: A Biography" that she "came to Carl Sandburg reluctantly." She had little respect for his work and thought of him as "timeworn, glib, chaotic, hardly worth notice in contemporary anthologies." Then she visited his North Carolina home and saw his "writer's workshop." Thus began what has evidently become a lifelong obsession, beautifully consummated in her children's biography.

Critics often rejoice that so little is known about Shakespeare's life, leaving them free to wallow in the work, but who can tell what a little more biography might do to a reading of the plays and the poetry? A.L. Rowse may have been wrong in his identification of the Dark Lady of the sonnets, but his critics missed the point: Inquiring minds do want to know; his was not a trivial pursuit. Or to put it another way, what would we not give to learn even a few more facts about Shakespeare? The best authors of children's biographies understand this hunger and do not apologize to their readers the way authors of "adult" biography sometimes feel they must.

*Ben Franklin's Almanac: Being a True Account of the Good Gentleman's Life* by Candace Fleming

Readers looking for innovation in biography ought to look at Candace Fleming's well-received and wonderfully titled book has an $18^{th}$ century ring to it, evoking the Age of Reason's mania for improving the mind and the material of everyday life. Ms. Fleming felt the conventional, chronological form of biography inhibited her from doing justice to Franklin's protean personality and awesome achievements. Like Ms. Niven, she works the life into a set of themes, which are copiously illustrated in a scrapbook mode that is rather like a child's version of composition. Ms. Fleming includes bits of Franklin's prose, etchings, sketches, cartoons, and documents; these lend a period flavor and, of course, are meant to mimic the style of "Poor Richard's Almanac."

I don't believe there is much of anything a biographer can do in biographies meant for adults that cannot be finessed in biographies aimed at the juvenile market. Certainly few subjects are too sophisticated for children to grasp. I tried to show this in my children's biography of Picasso (1993):

> He delighted in amusing his friends with simple pictures drawn on tablecloths and napkins on the same days he was creating human figures with exaggerated features (tiny heads and massive bodies) or with whole new anatomies, with animal faces, eyes positioned on one side of the face, and noses pointing in two directions at once—as if to say that modern art should create its own world and the artist should become his own god, presenting art not as a copy of the universe but as original, intact, and self-sufficient. Why not paint a nose pointing in two directions, since art, unlike life, can show the same thing in different ways simultaneously? For Picasso, art could be created with anything: a pencil, a paintbrush, a piece of rope, grains of sand, a clump of clay, a bit of cloth or wire. He was not afraid to experiment, and no material or subject matter was alien to his art. He believed that art could be equal to any situation; that is what makes him the complete artist.

I could tell that my editor wondered if I was not giving children too much of a workout, but I do not see why young minds should not be stretched. I did not, by the way, blink at the artist's misogynistic cruelty. I described Françoise Gilot as the "one woman he was never able fully to master. In one of his rages he did an unforgivable thing: he crushed a burning cigarette on her cheek, leaving a scar. Gilot did not flinch." "Adult" biographers often make some effort to rationalize or psychologize such actions; I think it is best not to play that game with children.

I favor biographers like Ann Waldron, whose lively biographies, "Claude Monet: 1st Impressions" (1991) and "Francisco Goya: 1st Impressions" (1992), remain in print. As other reviewers have noted, she is fun to read for the sheer pleasure of her prose. Profusely illustrated, her books are a bargain compared to the higher-priced and bloated studies produced by art historians. Ms. Waldron is also a pioneer, having produced the first biography of Monet for young readers.

But I would be remiss in concluding this column without acknowledging the contemporary master of biography for children. I first became aware of Newbery Award winner Russell Freedman when I watched him give a talk broadcast on C-Span. I was astonished at the depth of his research. Unlike most writers of children's biography, he does not cobble together his narratives from other biographies, but does original research. I was riveted by his story of visiting Louis Braille's house in France and his many other accounts of firsthand encounters with his sources. I called him up and invited him to speak to my class of Baruch College education students, who were earning degrees that would put them in New York City classrooms. In preparation, I had asked the students to write biographies of their own; he treated them as fellow writers, often asking pointed questions about how they planned to begin their books. Here are two Russell Freedman first paragraphs:

> No one had ever seen what Amos Root saw on that September afternoon in 1904. Standing in a cow pasture near Dayton, Ohio, he looked up and watched a flying machine circle in the sky above him. He could see the bold pilot lying face down on the lower wing, staring straight ahead as he steered the craft to a landing in the grass.—"The Wright Brothers: How They Invented the Airplane" (1994)

> Eleanor Roosevelt never wanted to be a president's wife. When her husband Franklin won his campaign for the presidency in 1932, she felt deeply troubled. She dreaded the prospect of living in the White House.—"Eleanor Roosevelt: A Life of Discovery" (1993)

Mr. Freedman's Eleanor Roosevelt biography is my favorite. Who would not want to know more after that bold first paragraph? But surely "Acrobats of God," the first chapter of "Martha Graham: A Dancer's Life" (1998), opens just as felicitously:

As an ambitious young woman who wanted to create a new kind of dance, Martha Graham spent many hours at New York City's Central Park Zoo. She would sit on a bench across from a lion in its cage and watch the animals pace back and forth, from one side of the cage to the other. She was fascinated by the elemental power of the lion's great padding steps, by the purity of its movements. Again and again, it took four steps across the cage, turned in "a wonderful way" then took four steps back. "Finally, I learned how to walk that way," Graham recalled. "I learned from the lion the inevitability of return, the shifting of one's body."

Tell me, is there a biographer, writing for adults or children, who can do better than this?

# Chapter Eight

# *Innovative Biographies*

*Pocahontas: Medicine Woman, Spy, Entrepreneur, Diplomat* by Paula Gunn Allen

At last, here is a biography accompanied by blurbs that do not praise it highly enough. To be sure, this is a "first rate biography…brilliantly written" with "some shocks" culminating in a "creative assessment of history and myth." But "Pocahontas" is nothing less than a watershed event in the historiography of the Americas—not to mention one of the wittiest and wisest biographies I have ever read.

Paula Gunn Allen has endowed biography with a new backbone. She has found a way to strengthen the genre in just those places where it has seemed weakest. Many biographies sever the individual from the "biota, or life system, within which she lives and from which she derives her identity," Ms. Allen writes, and thus produce a biographical subject who is a victim or an oppressor, or who is given a "value and prestige above the rest."

Ms. Allen, on the other hand, restores Pocahontas to her Algonquin universe, "looking to it to explain her motives as well as describe her actions." The Jamestown fable about the Indian maiden who threw herself on John Smith's body to prevent his certain beheading by hostile savages has been transformed into the story of a precocious Native American priestess, possessor of a "dream-vision."

It has long been recognized that John Smith aggrandized his own part in the founding of Jamestown and that he sentimentalized his dealings with Pocahontas and the Powhatans, "people of the dream-vision." But Ms. Allen is the first biographer to radically reorient the romantic story to encompass, instead, the Joan of Arc-like magnificence of a woman who saw in the events of her own life momentous changes predicted not only in Powhatan lore but in the mythologies of most American indigenous peoples at the time.

Although Ms. Allen's biography is highly speculative, and she acknowledges the scant evidence directly revealing Pocahontas's motivations, her evocation of the Powhatan world is so powerful that Smith's and subsequent historians' versions of what happened seem no longer tenable. This is a very rare event in the history of biography, and it is exhilarating to read a biographer breaking down a foundation narrative and then reconstituting it. After "Pocahontas," one must reread Smith, his contemporaries, and subsequent scholars in the light of Pocahontas's world view.

The excitement begins with Ms. Allen's discussion of the name "Pocahontas," the meaning of which has never been definitively established. It was a nickname for Matoaka, a rambunctious young girl who did cartwheels around the fort the English settlers established in the early 1600s. The English thought of this 11- or 12-year-old as "wanton." Intensely curious by nature, she also belonged to a class of Powhatan women privileged because of their shamanistic gifts. If Pocahontas welcomed the English, Ms. Allen surmises, it was partly to discover the sources of their own powerful magic in order to report back to her own people. Pocahontas was not the first woman, she notes, whom Native Americans used as a spy.

Like many double agents, motivations were complex—no less complex than those of, say, Kim Philby, who remained an Englishman and a traitor in the service of what he regarded as a dawning new world. Even though we know much less about Pocahontas, Ms. Allen makes it impossible to ever again think of her as some kind of pawn in a clash of ideologies and cultures.

Instead, Pocahontas was the pivot point of that world, marrying at 17 or 18 tobacco planter John Rolfe and establishing America's first tobacco plantation—an accomplishment the couple parlayed into audiences with the king and queen of England. They made a heady entry into English society, in which Pocahontas, now Lady Rebecca and a convert to Christianity, served as a diplomat representing not only her own people but also the interests of the English company that had founded Jamestown.

Not incidentally, the company was looking to make her a brand name far more powerful than, say, Martha Stewart could ever have become. I invoke the names of our contemporaries to suggest just how apposite Pocahontas's story remains. As one of Ms. Allen's blurbsters puts it: "What appears to be a book about the past turns out to be a book about ourselves."

Ms. Allen acknowledges that her book is a "mixed-breed or hybrid life, as American Indian life in the United States is a mixed-breed or hybrid life, as I, the author, am a mixed-blood, hybrid woman" (for the record, she is part Native American, part Scottish, and part Lebanese). The biographer writes in a language that is "about as foreign as it can be to the reality the subject lived in," making the biographer's task "a tricky operation." That she surmounts the difficulties of what she calls only "an honest beginning" is apparent in the way her perspective oscillates between past and present, and between Algonquin and Anglo-American consciousness.

To Ms. Allen, Pocahontas took as much as she received from John Smith & Co: "I believe we do great injustice to pathfinders such as Pocahontas by discounting their massive contributions to the modern world and instead considering them as having lived tragic lives, victims of European greed." Even the greed gets new scrutiny in Ms Allen's admiring account of European adventurers seeking "a land where people were healthy, where peace reigned, where immortality was a given. It was this dream that energized most of them; the money-making part was how the dreamers convinced those in power that exploring was allowed."

The world was changing for both Europe and Native America, and Pocahontas, who died in England at the age of 20 or so, was "in a remarkable number of ways the living embodiment of this dual cultural transformation."

I read "Pocohontas" with rising excitement. This is biography as a book of revelations.

*I Am Alive and You are Dead: The Strange Life and Times of Philip K. Dick* by Emmanuel Carrère

If Emmanuel Carrère is right that "in a far more radical way than any of his contemporaries" Philip K. Dick has "effectively abolished the line between life and literature," then the biographer has found the perfect subject. "This is a book about the mind," Mr. Carrère announces, one in which he is attempting nothing less than a "trip into the brain of a man who regarded even his craziest books not as works of the imagination but as factual reports."

The biographer's claim seems preposterous; biographers are not clairvoyant. But consider the subject: Philip K. Dick wrote stories and novels that suggest brains are indeed permeable membranes and that you can imagine that what I imagine is true. If a biographer took his subject's epistemology to heart—as Mr. Carrère does—then it is not quite so outlandish to portray the biographer as the man with two brains. After all, Dick was an unconventional writer who believed, as Plato did, that this world is actually only a simulacrum (a word that often appears in this biography) of a more perfect universe, and perhaps of its sinister creator, who controls the world we think we live in.

Why shouldn't a writer as unorthodox as Dick merit a quirky biography? Mr. Carrère dispenses with notes, bibliography, and even photographs of his subject (although the biographer describes a few snapshots and the jacket cover has an image of Dick in dark sunglasses). These omissions are not the result of laziness or disregard for the conventions of biography—indeed the biographer is scrupulous about disclosing instances in which he has no evidence and cannot enter his subject's consciousness. But the absence of such trappings constitutes an acknowledgement that au fond biography is a work of the interpretive imagination.

I was disappointed to see that the book did not even have an index, but then I began to think about what indexes do to books: They chop them up into data. Isn't there a powerful reason why novels do not have indexes? Wouldn't an index be useful in "Wuthering Heights," for example: "Heathcliff, mysterious origins of." But an index violates the imaginative flow and rearranges the narrative universe.

Mr. Carrère doesn't want you to carve his book up into information bits, or to use it to gaze at pictures. He wants to create a novel experience while playing by the rules of biographical narrative. The biographer's narrative is meant to put Dick back together, not sunder him apart as the paraphernalia of biography too often does; in the same way, Dick's novels claimed to be recovering a part of reality that no one other than the author himself seemed to acknowledge.

As Dick himself put it in a speech (part of which serves as epigraph to this biography): "Often people claim to remember past lives; I claim to remember a different, very different present life. I know of no one who has ever made that claim before, but I rather suspect that my experience is not unique; what perhaps is unique is the fact that I am willing to talk about it." A Philip K. Dick novel tells you that if you think an event has happened, in some sense it has. History offers no alternatives, but human thought itself is an agency of action not hindered by so-called fact.

UFOs are preposterous only to those who have not really thought about them, Dick implied, because UFOs have no place in their world. But what about those people who cannot conceive of a world without UFOs? (I knew a brilliant psychologist who believed in them and could mount compelling arguments for their existence although he had never seen one.) Dick, early on in his career, met a group of UFO true believers who—like true Platonists—considered his skepticism a form of ignorance. They sparked Dick's belief that each individual, including himself, inhabits a "very different present."

A telling moment in this biography occurs when FBI agents grill Dick about his radical wife, Kleo. Dick befriended one of his interrogators and began to challenge his epistemology. If I say I am not a Communist, wouldn't you take that as proof that I am one who is intent on concealing his subversive mission? And if that is your view, then how can you say you are judging me by what I do rather than by what you cannot see me do? The flustered FBI man began to read Dick's novels.

Such evidence of things unseen is beautifully explored in "Blade Runner," Ridley Scott's film adaptation of Dick's novel, "Do Androids Dream of Electric Sleep" (1968). The protagonist (Harrison Ford) falls in love with a replicant (Sean Young), a manufactured human being. The replicants are so real that elaborate tests have to be devised to detect them when they, in Frankenstein fashion, rebel and escape their creators' control.

What Dick thinks and feels as man and writer is richly developed in this riveting biography. Mr. Carrère is able to plumb his subject's psyche because Dick constantly circulated his ideas among friends, lovers, and wives—not to mention the letters he wrote to an improbable set of recipients, ranging from Richard Kleindienst (Richard Nixon's attorney general) to Linda Ronstadt (whose records, Dick sometimes thought, were addressed directly to him).

Yes, Dick was often on drugs (Mr. Carrère calls him a "chemical cocktail shaker") and was paranoid. But he was also able to dissect his paranoia in the interest of presenting a profound world view. This incessant talker (he liked to address God in Latin) was a visionary whose novels continue to shake up our world.

Mr. Carrère's book is mesmerizing. Seldom have I read a biographer who drew me so deeply into his subject's world. I have never read a Philip K. Dick novel, I must confess, but, boy, did Emmanuel Carrère make me want to drop everything and become—as he calls his subject's devoted readers—a Dickhead.

# Chapter Nine

## Comparing Biographers

*Under a Wild Sky: John James Audubon and The Making of Birds of America* by William Souder
*Audubon's Elephant: America's Greatest Naturalist and the Making of Birds of America* by Duff Hart-Davis

Both biographers begin their books in medias res, at nearly the same point: In 1826, John James Audubon sails to Liverpool looking for subscribers to his landmark elephantine volumes,"Birds of America," which the author carries slung across his back in a huge leather-bound portfolio, weighing perhaps 100 pounds. He is determined to produce a series of books that will contain life-size paintings.

Printers in America rejected Audubon's outlandish project not only because of the expense entailed in engraving and binding a work with such unprecedented dimensions (39 1/2 by 29 1/2 inches), but also because he was a nobody, entering the field late—a poor bet given that Alexander Wilson, a wily Scot, had already published "American Ornithology" and has the backing of important American naturalists.

Audubon does what other Americans do after failing to attract renown at home: He makes his reputation in England. Duff Hart-Davis emphasizes how the handsome 40-year-old, dressed as an American rustic but speaking a unique blend of French-accented English, wows the Liverpudlians. He is as exotic as his birds—and he knows it. As William Souder puts it, the English have always been "enamored of roguish explorer types."

Like Alexander Hamilton, Audubon was Caribbean-born and illegitimate. Unlike Hamilton, however, Audubon was not an early success. Poorly educated and bad at business, he was a fantasist, who in another era and in another genre could have accompanied Huck Finn on his raft, telling stretchers along the length of the Mississippi.

Whereas Hamilton said as little as possible about his early unfortunate life, Audubon refashioned his. His father had been a lieutenant in the French army; Audubon made him an admiral. Audubon so mystified his early years that he was rumored to be the Dauphin, the long lost son of Louis XVI and Marie Antoinette.

Curiously, while Mr. Hart-Davis acknowledges at the beginning of his biography Audubon's prevaricating side, little notice is taken of it once the biographer sharpens his focus exclusively on the great artist and his mighty determination to get his book published. One would almost think Audubon had reformed were it not for Mr. Souder's account, which shows that Audubon continued his habit of telling whoppers—fabricating a relationship with Daniel Boone, for example, that he knew his European audience would relish.

This life story, so full of color, deserves to be illustrated with Audubon's own gorgeous plates, which Mr. Hart-Davis's publisher does handsomely. Next to Mr. Hart-Davis's opulent yet relatively inexpensive book, Mr. Souder's seems a poor thing—both in terms of paper and pictures. What a pity, since both biographies have their merits.

Mr. Souder is amusing and informative as he exposes Audubon's claims to have studied with Jacques-Louis David. Mr. Hart-Davis points out that there is no documentary evidence to support Audubon's unlikely claim to this artistic pedigree, but Mr. Souder makes the even more telling point that Audubon's struggle to master oil painting (as opposed to drawing, for which he seems to have had an innate talent) makes no sense if he had studied with a European master.

Mr. Hart-Davis focuses mainly on those biographical details that illuminate the artist. By his teens Audubon was already mad about drawing birds. His father had sent him to America to learn the language and how to farm. But Audubon wanted to study nature, not master it—except, that is, for his lifelong passion for hunting. Mr. Hart-Davis provides the conventional explanation: Naturalists killed birds because aside from trapping this was the only way to study them. "This is wrong," Mr. Souder boldly dissents. Even if Audubon had binoculars and other modern inventions, he would still have shot birds—just as many naturalists do today, the biographer observes. This is just one example of Mr. Souder's fresh, unsentimental, and complex view of his subject.

Both biographers make perceptive comments on what made Audubon great. His pictures captured birds in action, enacting the drama of avian life. Before Audubon, ornithologists presented stiff, static poses of birds, which did not do justice to their variety or to their habitats.

Both biographers could have made more of the inspiration Audubon took from Sir Walter Scott and James Fenimore Cooper, whose narratives made nature itself into a character in their novels. Indeed, though Scott admired Audubon's pictures, he called them "stiff"—an observation neither biographer seems to understand. To the novelist, even the liveliest Audubon picture could not rival narrative's ability to portray the temporal. Audubon would sometimes paste his drawings of birds onto backgrounds an engraver or another artist drew, and I suspect this is what Scott sensed: There was a disjunction between landscape and creature that sometimes impeded the fluidity of the image.

On the other hand, as any birder can tell you, and what I have myself observed, no photograph—and perhaps no narrative—can match the greatness of Audubon's birds, because every drawing was based on a lifetime of observation. An Audubon picture is the essence of bird, not a snapshot, not an angle on a bird, but an eternity of bird, the bird itself. Whereas photographs are all about time, Audubon is timeless.

Mr. Hart-Davis's book has a wonderful plate showing how Audubon mounted his birds with wire and wood so that he could re-create their three dimensional world. Mr. Souder writes fascinating passages about the artist's technique, detailing how he skinned birds, for example. Honestly, I don't see how you can have one biography without the other.

## *John James Audubon: The Making of an American* by Richard Rhodes

Two excellent biographies of Audubon appeared in 2004. William Souder's "Under a Wild Sky: John James Audubon and the Making of The Birds of America" and Duff Hart-Davis's "Audubon's Elephant: America's Greatest Naturalist and the Making of The Birds of America." It seems necessary to ask, therefore, what Pulitzer Prize winner Richard Rhodes can add to this inspiring, if often told, story.

Mr. Rhodes's publisher promotes his book as the first major biography in forty years, adding: "Here is a revelation of Audubon as the major American artist he is. And here he emerges for the first time in his full humanity—handsome, charming, volatile, ambitious, loving, canny, immensely energetic." Certainly Mr. Rhodes's book is longer than both Souder's and Hart-Davis's, but Mr. Rhodes's portrayal of Audubon himself does not differ markedly from those of his immediate predecessors. And unfortunately Mr. Rhodes himself does not explain how he sees his book in the context of the voluminous literature—biographical and otherwise—about Audubon.

But it is not facts but narrative drive that distinguishes Mr. Rhodes from Souder and Hart-Davis. Mr. Rhodes is especially adept at rendering the every day concerns of his subject, the intricate concatenation of events that led to the publication of Audubon's classic book, with (toward the end of the biography) summative passages that convey why Audubon is both a great American and a great artist.

Mr. Rhodes begins his biography by being true to his subtitle: "The sharp cries of gulls wheeling above the East River docks welcomed the handsome young Frenchman to America." Birds, the biographer implies, do not merely become Audubon's subject, they represent the freewheeling America that this emigrant embraces and forges into a new identity.

Perhaps because Souder and Hart-Davis focus like art historians and critics upon Audubon's achievement, their books begin in *medias reas:* In 1826, John James Audubon sailed to Liverpool looking for subscribers to his landmark elephantine volumes, "Birds of America," which the author carried slung across his back in a huge leather-bound portfolio, weighing perhaps a hundred pounds. He was determined to produce a series of books that would contain life-size paintings.

Printers in America rejected Audubon's outlandish project not only because of the expense entailed in engraving and binding a work with such unprecedented dimensions (39 1/2 by 29 1/2 inches), but also because he was a nobody, entering the field late—a poor bet given that Alexander Wilson, a wily Scot, had already published "American Ornithology" and had the backing of important American naturalists.

Then Audubon did what other Americans have done after failing to attract renown at home: He made his reputation in England. Duff Hart-Davis emphasizes how the handsome 40-year-old, dressed as an American rustic but speaking a unique blend of French-accented English, wowed the Liverpudlians. He was as exotic as his birds—and he knew it. As William Souder puts it, the English have always been enamored of roguish explorer types.

Mr. Rhodes begins his biography by being true to his subtitle: "The sharp cries of gulls wheeling above the East River docks welcomed the handsome young Frenchman to America." Birds, the biographer implies, do not merely become Audubon's subject, they represent the freewheeling America that this emigrant embraces and forges into a new identity.

Mr. Rhodes does not approach this part of Audubon's biography until Part Three (p. 249). Until then, the frenetic, resourceful yet unsuccessful Audubon is seen schooling himself in the habitats of America, making do with farming and various other businesses, and painting portraits of the prominent, while always remaining faithful to his dream of drawing and writing his epic story of America's birds.

By this long delaying action (delaying that is to those who are eager to discover how Audubon was ultimately able to realize his dream) Mr. Rhodes risks trying his readers' patience. That he succeeds is due, in large part, to the fact that he quotes copiously from Audubon's letters and other writings. Audubon's gift to all his biographers is the lengthy letters he wrote to his wife, discussing his travels and quarreling with her about his plans, but always sharing his confidences with a deeply loving and loyal mate. There are times when a biographer simply has to stand back, so to speak, and let his subject tell the story, and Mr. Rhodes does so with consummate esthetic tact.

The details about Audubon's early life emerge gradually in Mr. Rhodes's narrative—a good way to handle material that often makes readers fretful, those eager to get on to the important aspects of the subject's life. By his teens Audubon was already mad about drawing birds. His father had sent him to America to learn the language and how to farm. But Audubon wanted to study nature, not master it.

Or rather, Audubon wanted to take command of nature in his drawings and paintings. His artistic ambition was nothing less than Napoleonic. He aspired to equal the work of Jacques-Louis David, whose epic paintings are the quintessential expression of the Napoleonic period and of imperial desire. (Indeed, Audubon said he studied with David—an assertion all of his recent biographers dispute.)

Mr. Rhodes alone, however, explores the deeper truth of Audubon's attachment to David. In his birds, Mr. Rhodes argues, Audubon portrayed the "equivalence of ambition, passion, violence, endurance, even of good and evil between the animal world and the human." The biographer is well aware that this equivalence has been rejected as anthropomorphic. On the contrary, Mr. Rhodes replies, Audubon's "supposed anthropomorphism is an attempt to recover meaning, a system for translating the alien experience of a different animal order into human terms and parallels." The biographer then shows in his own relentless and persuasive prose how Audubon created this world:

> Thus his passenger pigeons ecstatically billing, sharing in their passion the crop milk they also make for their young. Thus his house wrens nesting in a hat, an image of tender family life that the hat's startling splash of bird shit bleaches of sentimentality. Thus his ferruginous thrushes (brown thrashers) defending their nest and nestlings against a blacksnake, the birds of all ferocity and the snake warily testing the air with its tongue.

The vivid imagery of this passage (notice that it is really poetry in prose, composed of lines, not sentences) is reminiscent of Whitman and indeed suggests exactly how Audubon made himself into an all-encompassing American by means of his close observations and energetic travels.

Even better is Mr. Rhodes's description of Audubon's golden eagle, its "talon piercing the northern hare's eye," which he later links to a comment on the "larger world of animals." Classifying naturalists might object to Audubon's art, but Rhodes in rebuttal sees that the golden eagle "*was* Napoleon *and* his horse." This is sensational biography, buttressed by color plates that clinch Rhodes's point. There side-by-side his book reproduces David's magnificent painting of "Bonaparte Crossing the Saint-Bernard"—a study in dynamism, with the horse rearing up as Napoleon's right arm shoots upward, mimicking the diagonal composition of the painting—and Audubon's "Golden Eagle" ascending on the diagonal, the hare as surely clutched in the eagle's talon as Napoleon's horse is girdled by his flexed left leg.

Mr. Rhodes quotes Audubon's response to critics who called him unscientific for not classifying birds as his predecessors had done: Audubon explained that his aim was not to be systematic, for nature did not presents its birds to him in that fashion. He was evoking a whole world, not compartmentalizing it. Or as Mr. Rhodes puts it, Audubon "was not producing a catalogue but a work of art." His book was a "visual tour through the lives of birds as well as a series of separate scenes. Turning the pages of his book the reader would experience something like the "videos and films that people watch today."

And on one other important point, Rhodes has a fresh insight. Biographers have often called Audubon a poor businessman. True, he failed at farming and other businesses, but as Rhodes convincingly demonstrates, his subject was often the victim of market conditions that Audubon was powerless to change. Far more significant is the fact that Audubon produced *Birds of America* at a cost of $115,640 ($2,141,000 in today's dollars). He had no government grants. He made money exhibiting his work, selling book subscriptions, and bird skins. He traveled the world personally soliciting subscribers. As Rhodes concludes, "When he set out to create a work of art with his own heart and mind and hands, he succeeded—a staggering achievement, as if one man had single-handedly financed and built an Egyptian pyramid."

*Napoleon: For and Against* by Pieter Geyl
*The Life of Napoleon* by J. Holland Rose
Napoleon's Road to Glory: Triumphs, Defeats & Immortality by David Markham
*Napoleon: His Wives and Women* by Christopher Hibbert
*Napoleon: A Biography* by Frank McLynn
Napoleon: A Penguin Life by Paul Johnson
*Napoleon: A Political Life* by Steven Englund

"I cannot claim to be an expert on Napoleon. To do so rightfully one must have devoted a lifetime of study to the man and to the period," wrote the distinguished historian Pieter Geyl in "Napoleon: For and Against" (1949), a classic historiographical study. "An apology seems to be called for from anyone who gives to the world a new Life of Napoleon I," wrote J. Holland Rose in his still vital "The Life of Napoleon I" (1901, 1912, reissued in 2003 in an Elibron Classics two-volume paperback edition).

More than a hundred years later biographers and historians have not let up. Indeed, J. David Markham, "Napoleon's Road to Glory: Triumphs, Defeats & Immortality" repeats the claim that more has been written about Napoleon than any other historical figure. So why another? In Mr. Markham's case, he does not say, except to make clear that his own obsession began with his father telling him stories about Napoleon. A leading light in the International Napoleonic Society, Mr. Markham has produced a lively and lucid life that I would recommend to beginners in Napoleoniana.

But Mr. Markham brings us no nearer to answering "Why Napoleon?"—except for the biographer's subtitle, which evokes the romantic, tragic, fairy tale life of a figure that lends himself to narrative. Such descriptors help to explain why professional biographers favor Napoleon. They can break off and serve up juicy slices of life—just as the always engrossing Christopher Hibbert does in "Napoleon: His Wives and Women." Or they can synthesize the latest scholarship in a lively well-balanced narrative—as Frank McLynn does in "Napoleon: A Biography."

The urge to debunk Napoleon, to ruin him for those who love narratives of great battles and hymns to world historical heroes, is the impulse behind Paul Johnson's "Napoleon: A Penguin Life." This biographer presents a stark, tendentious version of the traditional attack on the Napoleonic era as precursor of the Hitlerian police state. But one does not have to be a Bonapartist—in fact one can even share some of Mr. Johnson's opinions (Geyl saw certain affinities between Hitler and Napoleon)—to reject his work.

If I had to choose one book to illustrate what not to do in a biography it would be Mr. Johnson's. He presents Napoleon as only a monster of egotism, a man so wrapped up in himself that he could not conduct a conversation. He would ask questions but never listen to the answers. Power was his only motivation. In short, Napoleon becomes an effigy. There is not a shred of interest in the man. Mr. Johnson's book is the most deeply dissatisfying biography I have ever read.

It is probably Mr. Johnson's procrustean performance that heightens my appreciation of Steven Englund's "Napoleon: A Political Life," a powerful contribution not only to Napoleonic studies, but also to the genre of biography. Like Mr. Markham, Mr. Englund grew up with a rather romantic vision of Bonaparte, which his leftleaning family made fun of. That romance remains an element in the mature man's outlook. Keenly aware of the "for and against tradition" that Geyl analyzed so shrewdly, Mr. Englund is on the side of the fors.

Mr. Englund often quotes J. Holland Rose, who put the case for Napoleon as a supreme political being. In his preface to the first edition of his biography, Rose first quotes Napoleon's comment, "Je n'aime pas beaucoup les femmes, ni le jeu: je suis tout à fait un être politique," and then observes:

> In dealing with him as a warrior and statesman, and in sparing my readers details as to his bolting his food [one of Mr. Johnson's favorite topics], sleeping at concerts, and indulging in amours where for him there was no glamour of romance, I am laying stress on what interested him most—in a word, I am taking him at his best.

Like Rose, Mr. Englund writes of the domestic, everyday man and lover sparingly, although with keen perception—as in the astute paragraphs he devotes to Napoleon's Polish lover, Countess Marie Walewska, one of the few females with whom the emperor discussed policy. If she did not materially affect his actions with respect to Poland, she certainly sharpened his perceptions of the role Poles could play in changing the map of Europe by helping to annihilate the ancien régime.

Readers of biography and devotees of Bonapartism will early on be refreshed by Mr. Englund's bracing style and point of view:

> For want of material to paint a complete portrait of the young Napoleon, one should refrain from speculating that the boy possessed any of the traits assigned him in their extreme form. Child Napoleon stood out in his family for his intellectual talents and willful character, but he was not an apparent genius, megalomaniac, or neurotic. I do not see deep-seated conflict or neurosis lodged in the boy Napoleon that explain or even shed much light on his later behavior. Here was not a psychologically hobbled man or a fascinating case of child psychopathology. Napoleon was, overall, I think, a rather bold, brave, and turbulent boy whom it was probably easy to love—and readily exasperating.

Biographers are wont to reduce politics to psychology; not Mr. Englund.

Mr. Englund's Napoleon has a strong sense of family, a keen but limited interest in the other sex, and above all an insatiable appetite for politics, fed by avid reading of both the classics and his contemporaries. He is a genius at making war and resorts to war too readily, Mr. Englund believes, but it is the organization of society and the question of who should rule the world that commands

Bonaparte's attention, and this is why he will always be the cynosure of biographers and historians.

Napoleon's belief that he could summon the forces that would change history, and the nexus—however problematic—between him and the French Revolution, constitute what Mr. Englund calls a "magnitude of hope" that has shrunken in our own times after the failure of the Bolshevik Revolution and the fall of the Soviet Union. Such events that cut us off from the "huge emotional investment that the late eighteenth-century 'party of hope' (Emerson's phrase) made." To reject Napoleon out of hand, Mr. Englund implies, is also to reject what is printed on our money: Annuit coeptis (a new beginning is declared).

Bonaparte is the herald of new beginnings. He believed in new worlds to conquer. Whereas Mr. Johnson ridicules Napoleon for selling off Louisiana, Mr. Englund shows him downcast with regret over the sale, which was forced upon him because of the need for money to combat his arch foe, Britain. Whereas Mr. Johnson sees only an engine of ambition, Mr. Englund portrays a man who wished to be in charge of history but was quite aware that the pressure of events dictated many of his moves. Indeed, when Napoleon fails, it is precisely because he thinks he can master contingency; too many unforeseen developments arise when, for example, he invades Russia. At such moments, he has forsaken his own political genius, according to Mr. Englund, rather than expressing a monolithic megalomania.

Mr. Englund demolishes much of the analogy between Napoleon and Hitler. Napoleon fought beside and inspired his soldiers. He never sought refuge or self-destruction in a bunker, and he surrendered himself to his enemies rather than attempt any sort of guerrilla action that might have resulted in a French Civil War. Although he used propaganda and cultural trappings to further his imperial designs, he was more Roman than Nazi in this respect, and the number of political prisoners in Napoleonic France was miniscule judged by modern standards.

Even Napoleon's resort to war, Mr. Englund notes, seemed quite different to his contemporaries, brought up in the classical tradition that saw war as a way to attain glory and achieve legitimate political objectives. What made Napoleon an original was his galvanizing of the citizen soldier fighting a patriotic war, a warrior who felt ennobled by his cause. This aspect of modern war was decried then, as it is now, but it is hard to see how modern mass society can be mobilized in support of good causes without resorting to some version of the Napoleonic code.

A case in point is Napoleon's retreat from Egypt—often treated as one of his abysmal failures by those of the Johnsonian school. Why, though, did Napoleon's men continue to follow him even in defeat? Mr. Englund answers:

Now is when the situation of the French in Egypt becomes interesting for the student of biography....Like Xenophon leading his Spartans out of Persia, Bonaparte met the challenge head-on. With the troops, Bonaparte could by turns be grandiose—telling them, "are you forgetting that if I owe you my glory, I made you yours?" and implacable: "scorning their mutterings of mutiny and their officers 'ultimatums'" (leading one of their spokesman, General Mireur, to commit suicide). Yet he could also be stoic and patient. He stood silently while an angry engineer, in despair at losing his friend in combat, violently insulted him in public. Finally, he could be gentle. With the soldiers who were plague victims at Jaffa, Napoleon not only laid hands on them—against the strenuous objections of the doctors ("you must know Bonaparte very poorly to imagine there are easy ways to change his resolution or intimidate him with dangers," a leading physician, Desgenettes, said)—he also worked with the sick for a time in an effort to show them that the disease was not contagious (as of course, it was) and that he, Bonaparte, had no fear of it. It was important for soldiers, he felt, to show no fear.

This is a magnificent being, however great his failings, evoked in a great work of empathy by a deeply knowing biographer, who understands that he has not done it alone, and that his biography is built on the backs of other biographers. These he generously quotes in his epigraphs—the best of which, by J. Holland Rose, captures Napoleon's unquenchable appeal for the biographer and for readers of biography:

> To very few man in the world's history has it been granted to dream grandiose dreams and all but realize them, to use by turns the telescope and the microscope of political survey, to plan vast combinations of force, and yet to supervise with infinite care the adjustment of every adjunct.

One does not have to agree with Mr. Englund's assessment to appreciate that he has written one of this new century's towering achievements in biography.

*Franz Kafka* by Nicholas Murray
*Franz Kafka: Representative Man* by Frederick Karl
*Kafka: A Biography* by Ronald Hayman

The avid reader of biographies, and especially of Kafka biographies, will want to know what is new about Nicholas Murray's life of the enigmatic Franz Kafka. Unfortunately, Mr. Murray is not saying.

The biographer does not seem to have found any new material, and he makes no claim for a novel or provocative interpretation of the life or the work. Occasionally he sets up a straw man in order to have a version of Kafka to knock down:

> But to see Kafka as a quivering neurasthenic, someone who knows only how to suffer, would be a travesty. His quiet, reflective, solitary personality also diffused warmth, wit, a sense of pleasure in life, just as much as a consciousness of its pains. He had friends, he was part of a lively and stimulating circle of remarkable Prague writers and intellectuals; he was successful in his career and popular with his colleagues; he relished his escapes into the countryside and outdoor pursuits; he enjoyed a modest but enviable reputation as a writer even if his major novels were unpublished in his lifetime; and he was attractive to women and enjoyed their company. However much he was tormented by private fears and lonely anxieties, he was loved by all who came into contact with him.

So there! But whose Kafka is Mr. Murray challenging? Neither his notes nor his narrative say. And Mr. Murray himself rather undercuts this chipper paragraph later on, as he becomes mired in Kafka's—I have to call it so—neurasthenia. The Kafka of the fiction, diaries, and letters may have discounted his ebullient and enticing side, but the biographer does little to restore him.

Further on Mr. Murray dismisses the notion that Kafka was "either a practicing (or repressed) homosexual or a misogynist with a hatred of heterosexual sexuality....Kafka's difficulty with marriage was of a different order, and when he struggled with his own courtships he turned exclusively to women for support and understanding." With whom is the biographer arguing? Is this a prevalent view of Kafka that Mr. Murray is refuting?

Biographies of major literary figures ought to be cumulative, to provide the reader with a sense of where in the historical process a particular biographer enters. Mr. Murray does make a vague effort to help us place his work, observing that in the years immediately following Kafka's death he was viewed as a "quasi-religious writer, an allegorist of religious themes, a modern Everyman." Absurdists and existentialists abstracted and absorbed Kafka as one of their own—coining the term "Kafkaesque" to describe the menacing and meaningless world they found in his writings. But in the last half of the 20th century, Mr. Murray continues, a "more nuanced picture" has developed, which takes into account the writer's Prague background, his Jewishness, his intimate family, and romantic relationships. He has emerged as "a particular man in a particular place at a particular time."

This Kafka is the one Mr. Murray's biography presents. Good enough—except what about all those other biographies of the last half century? What about the late Frederick Karl's monumental "Franz Kafka: Representative Man," with its all-encompassing second subtitle: "Prague, Germans, Jews, and the Crisis of Modernism" (1991) or Ronald Hayman's thriftier "Kafka: A Biography" (1981)—to mention just two of a half dozen or so Kafka biographies that have appeared in English?

I'm especially fond of Mr. Karl's ambitious—indeed, over the top—tome because it is so relentlessly interpretative. At close to 800 pages his biography is not the kind of huge narrative that attempts to be definitive in the sense of settling certain issues once and for all. On the contrary, Karl is authoritative because he knows

> There are, indeed, several Kafkas, for he played many roles and was in his own eyes several people, perhaps even an imposter. There is the historical Kafka, born in Prague in 1883, dead near Vienna in 1924. There is Kafka who kept a detailed diary beginning in 1910 and who created through it, as it were, a second Kafka: the man observing the writer, the writer observing the man. Then there is the Kafka whose lengthy letters to Felice Bauer and to other friends and relatives reshaped the historical Kafka, as he play-acted for them, taking on a large variety of roles, none of which he knew he could actually play. In these letters we have Kafka's autobiography, and in the large group to Felice we have a spiritualized journey that we might call "spiritualized autobiography." There is, of course, Kafka of his novels and short fictions, who appears to observe the entire course of the twentieth century. This is the Kafka who has, so ambiguously, entered literary history. There is, still further, the Kafka of the piercing eyes that were aware of the internal disaster of his conditions as his body deteriorated from tuberculosis, and through those eyes a reflection of Europe burning itself up, as though caught by a gigantic disease. There are all these seemingly conflicting Kafkas, plus the man who worked well and efficiently, gaining frequent promotions, for an accident insurance firm, who suffered terrible digestive ailments and crippling headaches, who experienced most of his sexual release with prostitutes, who tried one bogus health cure after another, and who agonized through it all over every word he wrote.

This paragraph from Karl's preface does not only present a comprehensive view of a contradictory man. It also speaks to Virginia Woolf's notion that the biographical subject has many selves. Karl, in short, has given us a kind of primer by which to read both his biography and Kafka's. We know where both the biographer and his subject stand.

Karl writes what he calls "critical biography," by which he means a work that integrates the literary figure's writing into a portrait of the writer's many selves. He refers to Mr. Hayman's book as only "biographical." But Mr. Hayman certainly focuses on Kafka's work—indeed, he begins with a discussion of Kafka's story "The Judgement."

A sentence of Mr. Hayman's clarifies matters: "Kafka's whole life was a series of hesitations in the process of condemning himself and carrying out the execution." I cannot imagine Karl or Mr. Murray writing such a sentence. It compresses the different Kafkas into a single conceit, an organizing principle that allows the biographer to write deftly and elegantly. His is one of those 300-page biographies that the British in particular favor but that are hailed by relieved reviewers the world round.

Mr. Hayman's approach is good as far as it goes. It will not do to call him reductive when in fact that is what biography—or one form of it—is anyway. There is nothing wrong, to my mind, with an exclusive biographical focus. There are other ways to write biography—as Mr. Karl demonstrates without denigrating his predecessors—but the Hayman approach allows the biographer to concentrate with great intensity on what he believes is the governing law of a life.

Still seeking a sense of what might separate Mr. Murray from other biographers, I examined the way he treats Kafka's dying wish that all his unfinished and unpublished work be burnt. Mr. Murray finds the writer's instruction to his friend and first biographer, Max Brod, "exactly comprehensive and utterly unambiguous. Kafka at this time wanted to perform a kind of self-cancellation." I like that "at this time," for one aspect of Mr. Murray's biography that is skillfully pursued—whether or not it is new—is his sense of circumstances and of temporality. The self is shaped by contingency.

I was amazed, at first, that Mr. Hayman makes no comment at all about this wish. He just quotes it. But why comment, given the sentence of Mr. Hayman's I have already quoted? In his view of Kafka's motivations, every creative act implicitly leads to destruction. Kafka possessed a guiding sensibility that events cannot alter.

Then there is Karl, who comes back to Kafka's wish a half-dozen times throughout the biography. He implies that the writer's instructions to Brod were nothing but ambiguous—and purposely so. This biographer invokes the terrible looming figure of the father, who never took the slightest interest in his son's writing and who, in his son's words, becomes the very voice of defeatism. Kafka came to fear success, Karl suggests, invoking "The Judgment." This is why he told Brod to destroy everything: "The more things I was successful in, the worse the final outcome would inevitably be."

Later Karl links Kafka's destruction of his literary legacy with the doom of the Austrian-Hungarian empire, which was part of the writer's "vision of bleakness and blackness." Later still he challenges the thesis that Kafka was a perfectionist who could not bear for his unfinished novels to survive him. On the contrary, the instructions to Brod constituted an "act of pride," Karl contends, because Kafka had created a myth of himself. He was one of those legendary figures who see the world as dying with him; after his death "nothing else matters." Karl likens the very act of having a friend burn one's papers to building one's own funeral pyre. Even so, Karl adds, Kafka had to know that some of his published work would survive him no matter what he did. Like the ruins of ancient temples, his fragments further his mystique. Certain readers, I'll wager, would find Karl's plethora of interpretation distracting, too fussy and far-fetched. But I rather think he is right—or, rather, that he is adept at playing Kafka's game, which is, in part, a big tease.

This is certainly all too much for Mr. Murray, who believes in the fullness of time and in cutting out the middlemen. For him his narrative is sufficient unto itself, and his biography comes to a Kafkaesque conclusion, anchored in a historical fact: Many of those close to the writer met their ends in the death camps.

*Inside George Orwell: A Biography* by Gordon Bowker
*The Unknown Orwell* by Peter Stansky and William Abrahams
*Orwell: A Life* by D. J. Taylor
*George Orwell: A Life* by Bernard Crick
*George Orwell: The Authorised Biography* by Michael Shelden
*Orwell: Wintry Conscience of a Generation* by Jeffrey Meyers
*George Orwell* by Scott Lucas
*The Girl From the Fiction Department: A Portrait of Sonia Orwell* by Hilary Spurling

Consider this a column on the protocols of Orwell biography. To date, there have been seven biographies—not too many, I would contend, especially when you examine the biographer's rules of engagement in dealing with a life story that is already well known. Gordon Bowker, for example, begins with a preface cunningly designed to demonstrate that the all-too-familiar is, in fact, false—or at least askew.

It is now possible, Mr. Bowker argues,"for more attention to be directed to Orwell's quite complex sexuality and strangely deceptive nature." The straightforward George Orwell, author of the no-nonsense "Politics and the English Language," a deviant? Then there is Orwell's KGB file, which has recently become available and which gives a "clearer picture of how he was hunted and spied on in Spain." Our hero, it turns out, was even more menaced than we had supposed. But that is not all! There is an "exotic side" of the man "not fully portrayed in previous accounts of his life." I'm going to stop here, having cited half the claims for new revelations Biographer Bowker makes in his breath-taking preface, quoting only this sentence near the end of his pitch which makes me wonder if he is not writing a satire on the conventions of biography: "Most biographers like to think that they have turned up new and important information and been able thereby to cast their subject in a new light." Just so: By the end of Mr. Bowker's preface, it seems that there is not much in Orwell's biography that is not in need of some repair.

This is not to say that Mr. Bowker does not add much to our understanding of Orwell, but sometimes—as in the case of his vaunted new material on Orwell's ancestry—the details do not really signify, instead serving only to clog the narrative. D.J. Taylor, on the other hand, seems far less concerned about originality, suggesting rather that his account emerges out of a deep reading not only of primary sources but of the other Orwell biographies. I especially like his comments on the sometimes forgotten "The Unknown Orwell" (1972), which Orwell's widow Sonia opposed—even refusing the authors, Peter Stansky and William Abrahams, permission to quote from their subject's work. Not only was this first biography (which covered the years up to 1938) well received, Cyril Connelly commented that the biographers had recounted his part in Orwell's life with "so much tenderness and insight that I am often deluded that the writers were there."

Mr. Taylor is equally generous with Bernard Crick's "ground-breaking account of Orwell's life," published in 1980—the first biography to be based on full access to Orwell's archive. But I wish Mr. Taylor had been more forthcoming about how he thinks his biography fares when compared with those by Michael Shelden and Jeffrey Meyers, published in 1991 and 2000, respectively, instead of merely hailing them as "highwater marks." In his pithy biography, "Orwell" (2003), Scott Lucas is blunt and terse: Stansky and Abrahams provide a "provocative" reassessment; Mr. Crick's account borders on hagiography; Mr. Shelden is "thorough in research and scope, but limited in conclusions"; Mr. Meyers "reinforces the standard narrative."

If all seven are necessary, it is because each author is possessed of an inimitable style and unique sensibility. Mr. Bowker, to his credit, acknowledges as much: "different biographers, different readings, different portraits." Or, as I like to say: "The answer to one biography is always another biography." In this respect, George Orwell has been very fortunate indeed. Although Mr. Taylor and Mr. Bowker certainly have more material to work with than previous biographers had, the extent to which their books are better than Stansky, Crick & Co. can only be assessed in terms of the very biographies they are attempting to supercede.

Every biographer of George Orwell points out that the pseudonym for Eric Blair (1903–50) represents the effort of a writer to create his "personal myth" (Taylor), his "persona" (Bowker)—or, as Mr. Lucas puts it, Orwell's attempt to make of himself a "construction."

How little the man resembled the heroic myth is illustrated by a comic scene in Mr. Taylor's biography. The biographer goes to interview an "old gentleman named George Summers," who after "numberless digressions" describes his only encounter more than six decades earlier with Orwell, who tried to "worm his way" into the affections of Mr. Summers's then fiancée. Mr. Summers, riding a motorcycle, chased our hero, who was fleeing on foot from the attempted assignation. Apprehending his rival, Mr. Summers then pushed him off a bank on Southwold common, provoking Mr. Taylor to observe: "However incongruous, nothing in twenty years of reading and writing about Orwell has quite so narrowly conveyed to me what, in a certain sense, Orwell was like."

This is why Mr. Taylor sought out ordinary people "less touched by fifty years of posthumous sanctification." How St. George made his escape, or in what shape, the biographer does not say, and perhaps does not know. But the scene is almost fable-like in revealing the biographer's tenacious desire to turn up fresh material and to remind us that no matter how much we know about the biographed, we have more to learn. In this regard, Mr. Bowker earns back your investment with this intriguing opening to his first chapter:

> As a young man Eric Blair was fascinated by ghost stories and intrigued by black magic. Once, seemingly to deadly effect, he laid a curse on a schoolboy who had offended him. On another occasion he reported seeing a ghost. Later, he told a friend that he used a pseudonym so that no enemy could take his name and work magic against him. In dreams he looked for symbols and interpretations, and more than once had highly prophetic visions. None of this quite fits with the widely held image of a man who transformed himself into the writer of clear-headed, rational and lucid prose, George Orwell.

Similarly, the iconoclastic Mr. Taylor goes Mr. Bowker and other biographers one better by attacking Orwell's famous dictum, "Good prose is like a windowpane." Mr. Taylor points out: "One doesn't have to be a literary theorist to know that this is nonsense." A writer like Joyce (whom Orwell admired) hardly wrote transparent sentences, the biographer reminds us—but such statements, Mr. Taylor might have added, were essential to the creation of the plain-speaking Orwell persona. I almost think it might be possible to create an ensemble Orwell biography culling bits from the seven contenders. I would include, for example, this bit of Shelden:

> Mrs. Blair [Orwell's mother] was not a dull Edwardian housewife. She had an artistic temperament and liked to surround herself with fanciful objects—rainbow silky curtains, embroidered cushions and stools, ivory figurines, and small hand-covered boxes, full of sequins and beads. She was an amateur photographer and developed her own negatives. Though not a great reader, she appreciated good books and was curious about new ideas. Several of her friends were active in the suffragette movements, and her sister Nellie enjoyed a brief career on the stage.

How's that for compression? As an ordering of facts and impressions and pictures and cultural background in one paragraph, it cannot be beat.

Mr. Meyers includes helpful maps of Orwell's world and is adept at evoking the dull and shameful job his father Richard Blair held in the Opium Department of the British government in India. Richard supervised the poppy growers in his district and made sure they remained efficient: "As long as the money kept pouring in neither Richard nor the Indian government was greatly concerned about what happened when the tons of opium—illegal in India—reached the dope fiends in China." By the 1920s, Orwell "felt intensely guilty about his father's personal involvement in the most vicious and indefensible kind of imperialistic exploitation." The ensemble biography should work its way back to Mr. Crick, who can provide the therapeutic kicker, which should provoke a yen for yet another Orwell biography. Just when we believe we have mastered Orwell, we come upon this dire admonition:

> [R]eading a lot of "good biography" and beginning to grapple with the evidence for this book....I grew to be skeptical of much of the fine writing, balanced appraisal and psychological insight that is the hallmark of the English tradition of biography. It may be pleasant to read, but readers should realize that often they are being led by the nose, or that the biographer is fooling himself by an affable pretence of being able to enter into another person's mind. All too often the literary virtues...give rise to characteristic vices: smoothing out or silently resolving contradictions in the evidence and bridging gaps by empathy and intuition.

I am obliged to note that Mr. Bowker errs a bit in this direction when he resorts to what "must have been." No understanding of the evolution of Orwell biography can be complete without confronting the vexed history of the widow Orwell. Mr. Taylor and Mr. Bowker treat Sonia gingerly in the wake of Hilary

Spurling's recent memoir, "The Girl From the Fiction Department," which seeks to exculpate her friend. But Sonia destroyed some of Orwell's letters, tried to stymie his biographers through various ruses, and left his literary estate a mess.

Jeffrey Meyers does not mince words, stating that Sonia "queened it up in artistic circles" even as she queered the study of her husband's papers. Naturally her friends are aggrieved by such charges. I read several of Sonia's letters while researching a forthcoming biography of her friend Jill Craigie, and they are charming and solicitous. Sonia could be a wonderful friend, but some of her judgments were wildly off the mark—as I found in reading a letter from her to Richard Ellmann (now in his archive at the University of Tulsa), in which she doubted that the much acclaimed biographer of James Joyce could understand Orwell's cultural background. Does Sonia really matter? She does because seven biographers (so far) continue to unravel the evidence she tried to suppress or manipulate for nearly three decades following her husband's death. Stay tuned.

*Harriet Tubman: The Road to Freedom* by Catherine Clinton
*Harriet Tubman: The Life and Life Stories* by Jean M. Humez
*Bound for the Promised Land: Harriet Tubman, Portrait of an American Hero* by Kate Clifford Larson

There have been more than 20 children's biographies of Harriet Tubman, a runaway slave, conductor on the Underground Railroad, spy for the Union army, Civil War nurse, and women's suffrage activist. But the last Tubman biography written for adults was published in 1943, and while it and a few earlier works established the basic contours of Tubman's life, until now no scholar has made the effort to research fully the historical record, verify previous narratives, or separate the person from her inspirational legend.

Now there are three, and together these new biographies—each one buttressed by an army of academic blurbers—provoke several questions about the nature of the genre. Should biography be primarily a narrative narrowed to its taut essentials? Then read Catherine Clinton. Or should the biographer question and provide a running commentary on her sources? Turn to Jean M. Humez. Wish to have a little of both? Kate Clifford Larson admirably obliges.

Of the three biographers, Ms. Humez seems most bothered by the fact that Tubman could not write her own story. An illiterate, this Moses—called so because she alone out of all the runaways returned to the South to liberate hundreds of slaves and bring them North—depended on abolitionist friends, journalists, and biographers to spread the word about her remarkably courageous and admirable life.

Since Ms. Humez sees herself as another "mediating source" (a favorite term among scholars who worry about how the biases of others infect renditions of Tubman's life), she provides a long, fascinating chapter on "Harriet Tubman's Practices as a Life-Story Teller" and another on the "Core Stories for Harriet Tubman's Own Perspective." For anyone interested in how biographies are put together, this chapter is required reading. It shows how certain repeated stories became part of the Tubman canon and how crucial the biographer, not just the subject, is in the composition of biography and history.

Even better, Ms. Humez provides two more chapters, "Stories and Sayings" and "Documents," which contain many primary sources that readers may examine to assess what Ms. Humez and other biographers have accomplished in assembling their narratives.

But to read a riveting narrative, return to Ms. Clinton. She makes clear at the beginning of her biography that the analysis of sources so prominent in Ms. Humez's account has been conducted offstage, so to speak: "During the research for this book, I found 21st-century scholarship and family lore from descendents as useful as the conflicting published accounts of the 19th century. I have tried not to privilege one set of sources over another, and to weigh competing accounts, rival agendas."

The result is that the biographer's voice is strongest in this version of Tubman's life, and the biographer becomes, in R. G. Collingwood's characterization of the historian, her own authority.

A good example of Ms. Clinton's flair is revealed in her handling of John Brown, who extolled Tubman, calling her "General"—as well he might have, since her gift for intelligence work would have put her at the head of the class, far outstripping Allen Dulles and any other spook, male or female, I have ever read about.

For nearly a decade Tubman made slave-stealing trips into the South, but she was never caught and never lost a single slave in her care. Her intelligence work for Union officers during the Civil War was indispensable, and if Brown had had her by his side during his raid on Harper's Ferry, Robert E. Lee would not have made such quick work of quashing Brown's attack.

Ms. Clinton handles the Tubman/Brown connection in spare, reverberating paragraphs: "First and foremost, Tubman shared Brown's impassioned hatred of slavery, which gave them a strong emotional and intellectual bond. Tubman had long viewed slavery as a sin, but under Brown's influence, she came to perceive slavery as a state of war." But there is more to biography than fine writing, and this is where Ms. Larson does Tubman some service. Both Ms. Clinton and Ms. Humez note that—unlike Frederick Douglass and other abolitionists—Tubman did not shy away from encouraging Brown's violent plot or dismiss his plans for a rebellion as fantastical. They both accept the idea that at the crucial moment Tubman was either ill, incommunicado, or somehow out of touch with Brown when he attacked Harper's Ferry. Ms. Larson, however, envisions another Tubman:

> She may have decided that Brown's attack was doomed to failure; she probably knew he had few followers, leaving him incredibly vulnerable. Douglass had rejected Brown's scheme as unworkable, and perhaps Tubman, too, came to the same conclusion, and that it was better to feign illness than to endure Brown's disapproval. Her strong survival instinct may have protected her in the end. Nevertheless, her silence on this issue, even years later, may indicate a careful decision not to reveal the full extent of her participation in Brown's raid.

This passage is a remarkable instance of what one can learn from a biographer when she is speculating. Better than her two colleagues, Ms. Larson has captured Harriet Tubman's clandestine nature, so essential to her career as an intelligence operative.

Reading Ms. Larson made me wonder if Tubman is not, in fact, the greatest spy this country has produced. This is not a frivolous claim, especially not in an age in which the U.S. is waging a war on terror. Harriet Tubman knew how to ferret out secrets and to keep them secret. She knew when to be aggressive and when to lie low. She knew that some of her stories could never be told, in spite of the fact that she loved to tell stories and excelled in doing so.

Which brings me to a mystery that none of Tubman's biographers solves. Indeed, they do not seem to perceive this mystery at the heart of Tubman's life. Why did she remain illiterate? Here is Ms. Humez's comment:

> We do not know exactly why Tubman did not pursue the project of learning to read and write after the war. The most likely reason is that providing for her dependents took all of her time and energy in those days. Her age and physical condition, including the liability to seizure or sudden bouts of sleep [she had been struck and severely wounded in the head as a young slave]...may also have been factors.

Except for suggesting that a physical disability might have thwarted Tubman, this explanation just won't do. A woman as determined as Tubman could not only have learned to read and write, she could have, like Douglass and Harriet Jacobs, authored her own autobiography—or at the very least produced notes that a professional writer could have perfected.

Not learning to write meant that Tubman seemed to put herself at the mercy of mediating voices, no matter how much she could shape an interviewer's questions or dictate her own version of events. But, then, the spy's power and place in history depend in part on secretiveness—on floating stories and preserving, in today's parlance, "deniability." Because she herself provided no written record, Tubman could avoid being caught in a contradiction or a lie. Discrepancies could always be attributed to the mediators. Like the spy or the journalist, Tubman never wanted to give up her sources—as a result she was always the source.

Douglass once wrote to Tubman about how she worked in the dark and he worked in the light, how her activities would never be as well-known as his because so much of his life was spent in public speaking. There is every indication that Tubman was a superb platform performer, but publicity was not the kind of fame she sought, and self-promotion not the mission she felt called upon to accomplish.

It is no accident that so many children's biographers find Tubman irresistible. She ensured that it was mainly the bold legend that got into print.And so her biographers butt up against the bulwark Tubman so cunningly constructed, worrying about what the mediators did to her, when it was Tubman all along who controlled the process—winning, in the end, exactly the kind of biography she wanted.

*The Singular Mark Twain: A Biography* by Fred Kaplan
*Mr. Clemens and Mark Twain* by Justin Kaplan

Fred Kaplan understands that the answer to one biography is always another biography. His work turns "Mr. Clemens and Mark Twain" (1966), Justin Kaplan's justly esteemed biography, on its head. While professing great respect for his predecessor's book, Fred Kaplan nonetheless insists on a different perspective—as his title signals. Whereas Justin sees a rift between Sam, the Victorian moralist, and Mark, the imaginative iconoclast, Fred perceives that the "writer and the man, despite the two names, are a unified personality." Fred (related to Justin only in the brotherhood of biography) portrays a unified Victorian American to the extent that any human being can be unified, no more and no less complicated, let alone divided, than any of his contemporaries. His pseudonym does not embody an attempt to escape from his other self, or a fundamental internal division. Although he was a man of many inconsistencies, they do not add up to a split personality; on the contrary they are the expression of the usual way in which people in Western culture, particularly in the nineteenth and twentieth centuries, respond to the pressures of daily life and play out their multiple desires and allegiances.

This is a plausible, even a persuasive way to deal with a highly influential previous biography. I regard Justin Kaplan's biography as very much a product of the 1960s, a time when American society confronted its ambivalence about capitalism and imperialism and when individuals felt called on to declare pro- and anti-establishment positions. The world looks quite different now. Capitalism and imperialism continue to vex our political arguments, but for all the ruckus about Iraq and what have you, is there any doubt that most Americans have taken the Twain way and learned, like Fred Kaplan's subject, "to respond to the pressures of daily life and play out their multiple desires and allegiances"?

The scope of "The Singular Mark Twain" suggests that Fred Kaplan's work is on a par with that of his precursor. This is what I would expect from a writer who dared to write a comprehensive life of Henry James that compares favorably with Leon Edel's classic biography of the master. Perhaps Mr. Kaplan might next wish to take on James Joyce, thus making sure that Richard Ellmann is not without a rival. Biography, like so many human enterprises, benefits from competition. The genre itself becomes stronger so long as there are biographers who refuse to be daunted by their putatively definitive forebears.

For both Kaplans, Twain is an American writer who fiercely attacked the excesses of a capitalist economy, the fatwas of religious fundamentalism, and the racism of his fellow citizens. Both recognize in Twain's story the astounding growth of a small-town, prejudiced white boy, a nativist and Confederate sympathizer, who ended up bankrolling the brilliant memoirs of General Grant and excoriating anti-Semitism—not only in his own country but abroad. Twain became a world figure because much of his work exposes cultural bias everywhere (and makes us laugh at ourselves and others) while at the same time relishing what we have come to call a multicultural world. He traveled the planet delivering uproarious lectures on nearly every continent. Born in Hannibal, Mo., he was in good measure Huckleberry Finn; settled into a plush home in Hartford, Conn., he became, as well, a Connecticut Yankee.

But can the Kaplan Twains be made congruent? Answering the question is rather like determining whether the glass is half full or half empty. Take, for example, the biographers' treatment of Henry Huttleston Rogers—one of the "chief architects of the Standard Oil trust and, according to the common stereotype of that trust as all horns and tail, one of its arch villains," to quote Justin Kaplan. Fred Kaplan does not demur from this portrayal, but he spends less time on Rogers's reputation and more on what Rogers did for Twain, which was to prevent the highly successful author from investing his royalties in new inventions that always failed to work or to find a market. Until Rogers came along, Twain seemed bent on losing not only his fortune but his wife's considerable wealth as well. A grateful Twain, at one time his own publisher, went so far as to prevent an editor in his firm from even considering publication of a book critical of Standard Oil.

Was Twain a hypocrite? If so, Fred Kaplan does not say so, commenting only that one more book attacking the trust made little difference one way or the other. Although Justin Kaplan does not blame Twain for such behavior, he does characterize Twain's attitude towards money in a manner you will not find in the new biography:

> For Mark Twain, who all his life had plutocratic ambitions but at the same time believed that money was evil and created evil, there had to be a price for any alliance he would make with archetypal plutocracy. The representative of a broad spectrum of paradox, as a writer he stood outside American society of the Gilded Age, but as a businessman he embraced its business values.

Here the Kaplans part company, with Fred arguing that his subject is singular; that is, that Mark Twain never stood outside of American society—no matter what he said. He focuses on what Twain did, eschewing the older biographer's psychological rhetoric. Twain's actions as portrayed in "The Singular Mark Twain" belie the idea that "money was evil and created evil."

For me, Fred Kaplan's argument about Twain's oneness is clinched in his portrayal of Twain's wife, Livy. While preparing his writings for publication, Twain deferred to her literary sensibility, toning down his profanity and, sometimes, his vicious criticism of American society. Much of the darker Twain emerged in publications that appeared after his death. Was Twain a hypocrite? Not in Fred Kaplan's reading of the man, who wanted to command a world audience, who would pull a punch in order to win a fight later, and who understood that he would have an even larger audience after his own death. For that Mark Twain, we have his wife to thank—as well as Fred Kaplan's singularly excellent biography.

*Zelda Fitzgerald: Her Voice in Paradise* by Sally Cline
*Zelda* by Nancy Milford
*Sometimes Madness Is Wisdom: Zelda and Scott Fitzgerald: A Marriage* by Kendall Taylor

This is an advocate's biography. The biographer as advocate is a stirring figure, engaging in the rhetoric of rehabilitation and in the dynamic of rectification. An old story, in other words, gets refurbished. In this instance, justice is done to an abused woman, that crazy flapper Zelda, symbol of the Roaring Twenties—the victim, it turns out, not only of her husband, whom Sally Cline calls "ever self-serving," but of the biographical brotherhood (it is mostly men) who abetted the scurrilous Scott. Ms. Cline is not always so melodramatic, but her biography leaves the impression that the men done her subject wrong.

Ms. Cline enters the ring with very fast footwork, so that by the second paragraph of her introduction we learn that nearly everything written about Zelda has been a "legend" (the biographer's favorite word is used as a refrain throughout the book). Zelda has been portrayed as a vibrant personality, her husband's muse, and the symbol of a generation—all of which obscure the real woman, "a powerful painter; an original writer; and a ballerina who began late but achieved substantial success."

That Zelda's periods of productivity were fitful and abbreviated accounts for the primacy of legend: "Generally we credit art produced consistently and continuously, which provides us with a complete body of work by which to make judgements," Ms. Cline argues. "Generally," I suppose that this assertion is true, but it does not mean much in terms of literature, since any number of writers have made their reputations by writing only one great book—or even just one book.

Ms. Cline has seen more of Zelda's artwork than anyone else, apparently. It is just great, although how great she is careful not to say, and her book lets us down by reproducing almost nothing that would bolster the biographer's claim. Nancy Milford's "Zelda" (1970) and Kendall Taylor's "Sometimes Madness Is Wisdom: Zelda and Scott Fitzgerald: A Marriage" (2001) provide both more modest descriptions of Zelda's art and more reproductions of it.

According to Ms. Milford and Ms. Taylor, Zelda often said she had no friends, yet Ms. Cline insists Zelda had important women friends whom earlier biographers rarely mentioned. But Ms. Taylor does deal with this subject, and so does Ms. Milford—although Scott's daughter Scottie successfully coerced Ms. Milford (aided by biographer Matthew Bruccoli) into excising reference to Zelda's lesbian affinities from her published book. Ms. Taylor and Ms. Cline treat Zelda's fascinating relationships with the lesbian circle located in the Rue Jacob in Paris with fascinating sensitivity, although Ms. Cline is very stingy indeed in her half-dozen back-of-the-book references to Ms. Taylor's research.

Ms. Cline shines in her last chapter, when she shows what Zelda did in her last years after Scott died. Biographers have overdrawn the portrait of a pitiful, unstable recluse. Zelda remained productive as a painter (she had several exhibitions of her work). But Ms. Cline strains to keep Zelda sane, referring as briefly as she can to the fact that Zelda was institutionalized three times during this period.

Whatever quarrels I have with Ms. Cline, however, should not detract from her ability to make us rethink what happened to Zelda Fitzgerald. Like Ms. Taylor, Ms. Cline suggests that in several instances the treatment Zelda received for her mental illness did more harm than good. Electric shock destroyed her memory; injections of various kinds had side effects so debilitating that the cure was indeed worse than the disease; and there is strong evidence that one of Zelda's psychiatrists molested her. Ms. Cline goes beyond Ms. Taylor in suggesting that Zelda was misdiagnosed as a schizophrenic—a catchall term, anyway, especially in the 1930s and 1940s. Zelda may have been manic-depressive, Ms. Cline argues, citing testimony from Zelda's last therapist. But both Ms. Taylor and Ms. Milford make a good case for schizophrenia, especially given the fact that Zelda repeatedly suffered from hallucinations and heard voices—aspects of her illness that Ms. Cline mentions but does not explore. Ms. Cline notes but does not take seriously enough the long history of mental illness in Zelda's family—affecting even her stalwart father, at one time the chief justice of the Alabama Supreme Court.

The argument that Scott drove Zelda to madness by appropriating her life in his fiction (she was a model for Daisy Buchanan in "The Great Gatsby" and Nicole Diver in "Tender Is the Night") is not advanced by Ms. Cline's biography. Yes, Scott could be mean to Zelda, forbidding her to write about their mutual experience; yes, he was cruel to call her a third-rate talent. He should not have censored her. But he did not destroy Zelda or prevent her from achieving a greater reputation as an artist—that point is clear in all three biographies (even when Ms. Cline is busy chipping away at Scott's right to act as the authority figure in Zelda's life).

That Scott is to blame for Zelda's eclipse would seem to be the burden of Ms. Cline's comparison of Scott and Zelda and H. L. (Henry) Mencken and Sara Haardt. The couples were friends. Both men had wives who wrote. Henry encouraged Sara, giving her the creative space that Scott denied Zelda. But Sara was a professional writer before Henry married her, and husband and wife did not share the same subject matter. Scott was not merely a professional, he was a genius, and like many geniuses he was ruthless. He could not abide Zelda's poaching on his literary property. Of course, neither Ms. Cline nor Zelda see Zelda's literary activities as poaching. Fair enough, but Zelda never saw her writing as anything but a vehicle for self-expression; her aim was to create work good enough to publish. Scott, on the other hand, wrote for eternity.

He was wrong to think that anything Zelda wrote could diminish him as a writer, but his fury and possessiveness and tenacity about his material is shared by many literary geniuses, and unlike some of those geniuses (T. S. Eliot comes to mind), he never shirked his responsibility to his mentally ill wife. Even when Scott stole Zelda's words from her diary or wrote down what she said for later use in his published work, he was doing no more than countless other writers—from Shakespeare to Philip Roth—have done. How those stolen words were put into a new context made all the difference—the difference, say, between Plutarch and Shakespeare. Scott looked at Zelda and saw a woman of exquisite aesthetic sensibility (she gave him the title for "The Great Gatsby") who was an amateur.

Only in the dance did Zelda claim the ambition to be great. Ms. Taylor does a better job than Ms. Cline in documenting how early and persistent was Zelda's dream of becoming a prima ballerina. Zelda dispensed with the dream when she married Scott, but she revisited it at 27 when her marriage was falling apart and—having becoming known mainly as Scott Fitzgerald's zany adjunct—she needed to earn back her self-respect. Ms. Cline makes clearer than any other biographer how good a dancer Zelda was. Zelda could not be great, her teacher wrote Scott, because she had resumed her lessons too late, but she could have had a respectable career. Why, then, did Zelda not seize her opportunity? She had an offer in hand from a good ballet company in Naples, and she turned it down.

From Ms. Cline's account, it is clear that Zelda was afraid to go off on her own. She required her husband's approval. She had rebelled against a traditional Southern society, but she could do so only beside the man she loved. Better than any biographer before her, Ms. Cline shows what it meant to Zelda to be a Southern girl: a belle whom society licensed to flirt, a Scarlet O'Hara with a cruel streak who was nonetheless susceptible to a strong man she wanted to master and protect her. Scott Fitzgerald, a Civil War buff, tried to play the role of gallant suitor, but this weak man, who doubted his masculinity, was no Rhett Butler. Zelda refused the handsome Scott twice before marrying him, only acquiescing when she saw the likelihood that his early success as a writer would wrest her from a stifling Southern way of life. In New York and in other Northern climes, she could play the flapper he could master in literature, if not in life.

It is a pity that Ms. Cline's grasp of American literature is weak. She has Scott consulting Lillian Hellman about playwriting in the early 1920s, when Ms. Hellman was still a teenager and a good decade away from writing her first drama. Ms. Cline also gets the facts wrong about Faulkner, one of Zelda's important literary influences—a more serious mistake—since Temple Drake in "Sanctuary" (the novel Zelda recommended to stuffy Southerners) is also the daughter of a judge and is just as confused as Zelda about how she can come to terms with her rebellious streak. Only one Faulkner novel is listed in Ms. Cline's bibliography, and it is not "Sanctuary."

Although Ms. Cline's advocacy has its faults, I have seldom read a biography that I have enjoyed arguing with more.

*The House of Mitford* by Jonathan and Catherine Guiness
*The Sisters: The Saga of the Mitford Family* by Mary Lovell
*Diana Mosley: Mitford Beauty, British Fascist, Hitler's Angel* by Ann DeCourcy

What do the Mitford sisters call to mind? Gaiety, beauty, high society, gossip, controversy, and a family that lived by extremes. The six Mitfords made their mark on 20th-century literature and politics, beginning with Nancy (1904–73), the oldest, whose novels and biographies remain in print—a tribute, above all, to her gift for transforming her family into a comic myth, the story of a "backwoods peer and his vague wife," as Jonathan and Catherine Guinness put it in "The House of Mitford"(1985). Not much of what Nancy wrote about her family is true, but then her aim was to entertain and to shock. All families have stories to tell, but the Mitfords seemed to make everything into a story.

To read Nancy is to take life at full gallop in a setting complete with landed gentry, horses and hounds, debutante balls, dancing lessons, and goofy governesses. Jessica (1917–96), the second youngest, burnished the Mitford myth by recounting in her memoir, "Hons and Rebels" (1960), how one governess taught the sisters to shoplift. "Is that true?" an interviewer asked Jessica's sister Diana (1910–2003). "Of course not!" Diana replied. "Really! Jessica wants to amuse her readers and she simply invents!"

But the reason each new Mitford biographer—and there have been more than a dozen books so far—gives for publishing yet another book is that the family was so inventive and still so newsworthy. The family turned itself into a fiction and a public spectacle, a fact evident in their penchant for constantly renaming one another. David Bertram Ogilvy Mitford, Lord Redesdale (1878–1958), the growling, scowling, comic, tyrant-father of Nancy's novels was Farve, Forgy, Forgery, TPOM (The Poor Old Male), among other cognomens. His wife, Sydney Bowles (1880–1963), later Lady Redesdale, became Muv, TPOF (The Poor Old Female), and the Fem. Nancy, aka Koko, Blob-Nose, Natch, later became a resident of France and a biographer of French figures such as Madame de Pompadour. She was then known as The Old French Lady, and after the success of her novels, Octopus Untruth. Pamela (1907–94), one of the few Mitfords to lead a quiet, conventional, country life, got off easy with the appellation The Woman—although that was transformed into the whimsical Wooms or Woomling. Thomas (1909–45), the only boy, was Tud. Diana got shorted with Dina, Dana, Cord, or Nard, though Nancy called her Bodley (a reference to Diana's large head). Unity Valkyrie (1914–48) started out as Baby and graduated to Boby, and then Bobo, or the Boud, and later Birdie. Jessica was Decca to most family members, although she was Little D to her mother and Henderson to her sister Deborah (born 1920), who herself became Debo, Stubby, Swyne, and Nine (a snide reference to her supposed mental age).

What all this wordplay suggests is a family that was a world unto itself, which means it was a family that behaved in ways that startled the world. Only it is more complicated than that, since each family member used only certain names and not others for, say, Diana, who was Cord only to Jessica but Honks to Deborah. In other words, this was an internecine group whose humor grew out of conflict and rivalry. Family togetherness meant a squabble—often a hilarious one.

But as Mary Lovell remarked in "The Sisters: The Saga of the Mitford Family" (2001), in retrospect one family name "seems like an eerie prophecy which the fifth Mitford child had no alternative but to fulfill." Of course, Ms. Lovell is alluding to Unity Valkyrie, who tried to kill herself rather than become one of Hitler's war maidens. She had traveled to Germany at the instigation of her sister Diana, who in 1936 married British fascist Oswald Mosley in a ceremony hosted by Josef Goebbels and his wife. Diana outdid her husband in extravagant admiration for Herr Hitler, but Unity was a Nazi cheerleader, even publishing a letter in a German newspaper that identified her as a "Jew hater." Living up to her name, Unity dreamed of an alliance between Germany and Britain. War came as a refutation of her two years in Germany and of her understanding that she had persuaded Hitler to forego an attack on the West. She met the Führer on no fewer than 140 occasions and took liberties with him that not even his closest associates dared venture. After Britain declared war on Germany, she put her pearl-handled pistol to her head and pulled the trigger, causing brain damage and death eight years later when the bullet, still in her head, suddenly moved.

Diana spent most of the war in prison with her husband. The beauty of the family, she had already become a public figure by the early 1930s, having married the very wealthy Bryan Guinness and partied with all the brilliant figures in the Bloomsbury Circle. She caused a scandal by consorting with Mosley, a married man, and by avidly supporting his black-shirted, stormtrooper-like followers. Diana loftily dismissed the thuggish aspects of Mosley's recruits, blithely pointing out that they liked their uniforms because they obliterated class distinctions.

Diana to me is the most fascinating Mitford because unlike Unity she remained coldly sane about her political convictions. And unlike Jessica, who became a lively and livid leftist while denouncing the crimes of communism, Diana never recanted, never wavered in her view of Hitler as a great man. In Anne de Courcy's recently published "Diana Mosley: Mitford Beauty, British Fascist, Hitler's Angel," Diana—then well into her 90s, is quoted as saying:

> Knowing about the Holocaust absolutely did not change my perspective of Hitler....I don't think of him as the man who did that, I think of him as the man I knew, who wouldn't have been capable of that. If he became so capable, it was really a form of madness, which in a way is understandable if everything you've worked for is being ruined.

Where do you begin to argue with a mind like that? Dr. Johnson once said there is no point arguing with someone who will not concede what everybody knows. It reminds me of a highly regarded novelist who told me he just could not believe that Alger Hiss was a spy. Why? Because he knew Alger's son, Tony, a fine man. How could his father do such a thing? No, it was unthinkable. Why did Diana not know what Nancy, as early as 1935, knew about fascism, satirizing her sisters' political involvements in a novel, "Wigs on the Green" (1935)? And is there something Mitford-like in Diana's rigid consistency? Only two Mitfords were fascists, although Diana's mother retained some affection for Herr Hitler even as the war began. But it is not what a Mitford believes that matters, it is the fact that the world can be Mitfordized.

This point was brought home to me when I wrote to Diana on July 2, 1992, concerning my research for a biography of Rebecca West. Selina Hastings, Nancy's biographer, had told me that she thought Diana had known Rebecca. I mentioned this in my letter to Diana, and identified myself as a great admirer of Rebecca West's work. I cannot remember if I was deliberately provocative in writing this sentence: "I find a particular relevance to West's work just now—given what is happening in Central Europe."

Very quickly, on July 14, Diana replied, thanking me in her own handwriting for my letter and saying straightaway that she never knew West. In July 1956, however, she had published a long article in The European on West, which was later bound into a handsome book, "The Writing of Rebecca West" (1986). "The more I read about, and by, Rebecca West, the more I disliked her," were the opening words of Diana's attack. She held it against West that she was a bad mother, and she asked me in her letter if I had read Anthony West, who had made a career out of saying just how bad a mother he had had. Diana had wanted to write about Rebecca and Anthony, but "it would obviously have been libelous." West's novels were "very silly, snobbish and second rate," and her journalism "full of tiresome irrelevancies." Diana conceded that "Black Lamb and Grey Falcon" was West's "best book," but her "values are completely false." Although Diana had a harsh and narrow mind, she had exquisite manners, and I don't believe her parting words were perfunctory: "I am sorry to write such a 'negative' letter but if you get the little book you will read my opinion, for what it's worth."

The letter is breathtaking because it does not mention a word about the fact that even before Hitler came to power she was a notable anti-fascist. Yet the world in which Diana lived resulted in the conclusion that West's values were "completely false."

I do not mean to say, though, that Diana was demented when it came to politics. When I read her "little book," I was shaken because she did expose some of West's weaknesses, and I felt I had to spend a solid paragraph in my biography replying to those charges. And unlike Jessica, Diana did not choose her friends along political lines. She enjoyed very fond relations with many people who abhorred her politics, just as she never rejected Jessica or any other Mitford, for that matter, even though Jessica denounced her. I regard Diana as the most Mitford because she remained true to her family, which always seemed to her most united in quarrel.

By coincidence—if you believe in such a thing—I received a letter from Jessica just a few weeks before my exchange with Diana—as if Jessica meant to provide an antidote to her sister. As a biographer, I have never gotten an unsolicited letter from a prominent person (PP). The PP always awaits the biographer's supplication. But Jessica had seen my author's query in The New York Times Book Review, and she wanted to know who was publishing my West biography and when. She had written a review of Rebecca's last book, "1900," and enclosed the piece with a note saying she had never actually met my subject. How generous, I thought. How cheery. How engaging. I hoped to meet Jessica—really just for the thrill of talking to another PP—but we never managed to connect again. Now I still believe that Jessica was being helpful and encouraging, knowing as a writer herself what it means to get the PP's attention, but I also think that even in this small way she was making the world a little more Mitford.

# *Name Index*

Abrahams, William, 82-83
Allen, Paula Gunn, 64
Arbuckle, Roscoe (Fatty), 31
Aubrey, John, 3
Auchincloss, Louis, 39-41
Auden, W. H., 5
Bailey, Blake, 51-52
Banner, Lois, 24, 26
Barber, Michael, 3-4
Becker, Jillian, 26, 29
Benedict, Ruth, 24-26
Blount, Jr., Roy, 54
Boswell, James, 17
Bowker, Gordon, 82-86
Brands, H. W., 39
Cannon, Lou, 19-21
Carlyle, Thomas, 41
Carrère, Emmanuel, 66, 68
Caws, Mary Ann, 56
Cline, Sally, 91
Clinton, Catherine, 86
Coffin, William Sloane, 37-38
Collingwood, R. G., 87
Craigie, Jill, 86
Crick, Bernard, 82-83
Dallek, Robert, 45, 48
Dick, Philip K., 66-68
Disney, Walt, 29, 32-33
Disraeli, Benjamin, 42, 44
Doctorow, E. L., 33
Edel, Leon, 11, 24, 54, 90
Ellmann, Richard, 11, 18, 86, 90
Emerson, Ralph Waldo, 40, 77
Englund, Steven, 75

Faulkner, William, 33, 55
Fitzgerald, F. Scott, 91-94
Fitzgerald, Zelda, 91-92
Fleming, Candace, 61
Fowles, John, 6-8
Freeman, Douglas Southall, 54
Freedman, Russell, 62
Gavin, James, 3
Gellhorn, Martha, 1-3, 30
Giacometti, Alberto, 9-11
Glendinning, Victoria, 2
Goldstein, Warren, 37-38
Greene, Graham, 11-14
Guiness, Jonathan and Catherine, 94
Hamilton, Nigel, 45, 48
Hart-Davis, Duff, 69, 71-72
Hastings, Selina, 97
Hayman, Ronald, 57, 78, 80
Hellman, Lillian, 16, 94
Hemingway, Ernest, 1, 3, 50
Hibbert, Christopher, 74-75
Highsmith, Patricia, 14-16
Howard, Jane, 25-26
Hughes, Ted, 26, 28
Humez, Jean M., 86-89
James, Henry, 4, 11, 15, 24, 41, 90
Johnson, Paul, 74-75
Johnson, Samuel, 19, 37, 51, 60
Jouvenel, Bertrand de, 3
Jungk, Peter Stephan, 32
Kaplan, Fred, 89-91
Kaplan, Justin, 49, 89-91
Karl, Frederick, 78, 80
Larson, Kate Clifford, 86
Lee, Robert E., 54-55
Lewis, Roger, 17
Lord, James, 8-9
Lovell, Mary, 94, 96
Lucas, Scott, 82-83
Lukacs, Georg, 33

McLynn, Frank, 74-75
Mailer, Norman, 8, 29, 34, 38
Malcolm, Janet, 27
Markham, David, 74-75
Mead, Margaret, 24-25
Meade, Marion, 31
Medvedev, Roy, 41, 44-45
Medvedev, Zhores, 41
Middlebrook, Diane, 26-27
Meyers, Jeffrey, 82-83, 86
Milford, Nancy, 91-92
Miller, Arthur, 27-29
Mitford, Jessica, 94-98
Mitford, Nancy, 94-98
Mitford, Unity, 94-98
Monroe, Marilyn, 27-29, 34, 47
Montefiore, Simon Sebag, 41
Moorehead, Caroline, 1
Morris, Edmund, 19
Mosley, Diana, 94, 96
Mosley, Oswald, 96
Muggeridge, Malcolm, 5
Murray, Nicholas, 78
Niven, Penelope, 59
Oates, Joyce Carol, 34, 51
Orwell, George, 5, 82-84
Painter, George, 11, 57
Plath, Sylvia, 26, 28-30
Powell, Anthony, 3, 5
Proust, Marcel, 56
Plutarch, 2, 37, 46, 93
Reagan, Ronald, 19-20, 22-23
Remarque, Erich Maria, 49
Rhodes, Richard, 71
Richardson, John, 8
Rollyson, Carl, 3, 5, 7, 9, 11, 13, 15, 19, 21, 23, 25, 27, 29, 33, 35, 39, 41, 43, 45, 47, 51, 53, 55, 57, 59, 61, 63, 65, 67, 71, 73, 75, 77, 79, 81, 83, 85, 87, 89, 91, 93, 95, 97, 101, 105
Rose, J. Holland, 74-76, 78
Sandburg, Carl, 59-60

Schlesinger, Arthur M., Jr., 39-40
Shelden, Michael, 12, 82-83
Sherry, Norman, 11, 14
Souder, William, 69, 71-72
Sparks, Jared, 37
Spurling, Hilary, 82
Stahl, Jerry, 31, 34
Stalin, Josef, 41
Stansky, Peter, 82-83
Strachey, Lytton, 37
Taylor, D. J., 82
Taylor, Kendall, 91-92
Tims, Hilton, 49
Tubman, Harriet, 86-88
Twain, Mark, 52, 89-91
Vine, Barbara, 34
Waldron, Ann, 62
Warburton, Eileen, 6
Warren, Robert Penn, 20, 33
Waugh, Evelyn, 4
Wells, H. G., 3
Werfel, Franz, 33
West, Rebecca, 3, 97
Wilson, Andrew, 14-16
Wilson, Laurie, 9
Wilson, Woodrow, 39, 41
Yates, Richard, 51-52

# *Title Index*

Alberto Giacometti: Myth, Magic, and the Man, 9
Anthony Burgess: A Biography, 8-10, 17
Anthony Powell: A Life, 3
Audubon's Elephant: America's Greatest Naturalist
                    and the Making of Birds of America, 69
Beautiful Exile: The Life of Martha Gellhorn
Beautiful Shadow: A Life of Patricia Highsmith, 14
Ben Franklin's Almanac: Being a True Account of the Good Gentleman's Life, 61
Blonde, 34
Blood Doctor, The, 34
Bound for the Promised Land: Harriet Tubman, Portrait of an American Hero, 86
Brief Lives, 3
Buster Keaton: Cut to the Chase, 31
Carl Sandburg: Adventures of a Poet, 59
Children's Hour, The, 16
Claude Monet: First Impressions, 62
Collector, The, 7
Dance to the Music of Time, A, 3, 6
Daniel Martin, 8
Diana Mosley: Mitford Beauty, British Fascist, Hitler's Angel, 94, 96
Erich Maria Remarque: The Last Romantic, 49
Francisco Goya: First Impressions, 62
Franz Kafka, 78, 80
Franz Kafka: Representative Man, 78, 80
French Lieutenant's Woman, The, 6
Gellhorn: A Twentieth Century Life, 1
George Orwell, 5, 82-84
George Orwell: A Life, 82
George Orwell: The Authorised Biography, 82
George Orwell, Wintry Consicience of a Generation, 82
Giacometti: A Biography, 8-10
Girl From the Fiction Department, The, 82, 86
Giacometti Portrait, A, 8-10
Giving Up: The Last Days of Sylvia Plath, 26

Governor Reagan: His Rise to Power, 19, 22
Graham Greene: The Enemy Within, 12
Great Gatsby, The, 93
Harriet Tubman: The Life and Life Stories by Jean M. Humez, 86
Harriet Tubman: The Road to Freedom, 86
Her Husband: Hughes and Plath—A Marriage, 26-27
Homage to Catalonia, 5
House of Mitford, The, 94-95
I Am Alive and You are Dead: The Strange Life and Times of Philip K. Dick, 66
I, Fatty, 31, 34
Inside George Orwell, 82
Intertwined Lives: Margaret Mead, Ruth Benedict, and Their Circle, 24
John James Audubon: The Making of an American, 71
JFK: Reckless Youth, 45
John Fowles: A Life, 6
Kafka: A Biography, 78, 80
Life of Graham Greene, The, 11
Life of Napoleon, The, 74-75
Magus, The, 8
Margaret Mead: A Life, 25
Mr. Clemens and Mark Twain, 89
Mythic Giacometti, 8
Napoleon: A Biography, 74-75
Napoleon: For and Against, 74-75
Napoleon: A Penguin Life, 74-75
Napoleon: A Political Biography, 74
Napoleon's Road to Glory: Triumphs, Defeats & Immortality, 74-75
Napoleon: His Wives and Women, 74-75
Nothing Ever Happens to the Brave: The Story of Martha Gellhorn, 1
Orwell: A Life, 82
Quiet American, The, 32
Perfect American, The, 32
Pocahontas: Medicine Woman, Spy, Entrepreneur, Diplomat Pocahontas: Medicine Woman, Spy, Entrepreneur, Diplomat, 64
Revolutionary Road, 52
Robert E. Lee, 54-55, 87
Sanctuary, 94
Silent Woman, The, 27
Singular Mark Twain, The, 89-91
Sisters, The Saga of the Mitford Family, 94, 96

Sometimes Madness Is Wisdom: Zelda and Scott Fitzgerald: A Marriage, 91-92
Stalin: The Court of the Red Tsar, 41-42
Tender is the Night, 93
Tragic Honesty, A: The Life and Work of Richard Yates, 51
Under a Wild Sky: John James Audubon and The Making of Birds of America, 69
Unfinished Life of John F. Kennedy, The, 45
Unknown Orwell, The, 82-83
Unknown Stalin, The, 41, 44-45
What's Become of Waring?, 4
William Sloane Coffin: A Holy Impatience, 37
Woodrow Wilson, 39, 41
Zelda, 91-94
Zelda: Her Voice in Paradise, 91-94

0-595-33747-3

Printed in the United Kingdom
by Lightning Source UK Ltd.
106211UKS00002B/200